D0686332

Privatizing Fannie Mae, Freddie Mac, and the Federal Home Loan Banks

Privatizing Fannie Mae, Freddie Mac, and the Federal Home Loan Banks

Why and How

Peter J. Wallison
Thomas H. Stanton
Bert Ely

The AEI Press

Publisher for the American Enterprise Institute
WASHINGTON, D.C.

Available in the United States from the AEI Press, c/o Client Distribution Services, 193 Edwards Drive, Jackson, TN 38301. To order, call toll free: 1-800-343-4499. Distributed outside the United States by arrangement with Eurospan, 3 Henrietta Street, London WC2E 8LU, England.

Library of Congress Cataloging-in-Publication Data

Wallison, Peter J.
    Privatizing Fannie Mae, Freddie Mac, and the federal home loan banks: why and how / Peter J. Wallison, Thomas H. Stanton, and Bert Ely.
        p. cm.
Includes bibliographical references.
    ISBN 0-8447-4190-6 (pbk. : alk paper)
    1. Fannie Mae. 2. Federal Home Loan Mortgage Corporation. 3. Federal home loan banks. 4. Mortgage loans—Government policy—United States. I. Stanton, Thomas H., 1944– II. Ely, Bert III. Title.

    HG2040.5.U5E455 2004
    332.3'2'0973—dc22

                                                                    2004014734

10 09 08 07 06 05 04   1 2 3 4 5 6 7

© 2004 by the American Enterprise Institute for Public Policy Research, Washington, D.C. All rights reserved. No part of this publication may be used or reproduced in any manner whatsoever without permission in writing from the American Enterprise Institute except in the case of brief quotations embodied in news articles, critical articles, or reviews. The views expressed in the publications of the American Enterprise Institute are those of the authors and do not necessarily reflect the views of the staff, advisory panels, officers, or trustees of AEI.

Printed in the United States of America

Contents

Introduction and Summary

Peter J. Wallison

Why

The first question everyone asks about a project to privatize Fannie Mae, Freddie Mac, and the Federal Home Loan Banks (collectively, the housing GSEs) is, Why? This question has two levels. The first is substantive: The U.S. housing finance system performs very well, or at least adequately; there are few complaints; why do you want to change it? The second is political: Yes, there are problems, but they can be addressed through better regulation; why bother to privatize these companies when there is very little political opposition to improving how they are regulated and quite a bit of opposition to privatization?

The answer to both questions is relatively simple. The housing GSEs contribute little to the quality of the U.S. housing finance system, yet they create risks for the taxpayers and the entire economic system that cannot be adequately addressed by regulation.[1] A sound privatization program should solve both problems, providing an improved housing finance system and eliminating the risks that the housing GSEs—and particularly Fannie Mae and Freddie Mac—create for the taxpayers and the economy generally.

In this monograph, we propose a comprehensive privatization program, including a privatization plan that will eliminate the housing GSEs as government wards without disrupting the residential mortgage market, and a complementary plan for a housing finance system in the United States that will deliver benefits to homeowners that are at least equivalent to the benefits delivered by the housing GSEs, without the necessity for government backing. Legislation to implement this program is attached to this summary.

The Risks Created by the Housing GSEs

Financial Risk to the Taxpayers. When we speak of risks created by the housing GSEs, we are speaking primarily of Fannie Mae and Freddie Mac. The Federal Home Loan Banks (FHLBs) present some risks for the taxpayers and the economy, but these risks—which will be discussed later—are somewhat indirect and small compared to those associated with Fannie and Freddie. At the same time, the FHLBs seem to serve no useful purpose. Although their risks are small, their contribution toward fulfilling any reasonably necessary national goal is even smaller. On balance, the FHLB system should also be privatized.

The risks associated with Fannie and Freddie, however, are direct and immediate and of two different kinds: a direct financial risk, which derives from the federal government's implicit backing of Fannie and Freddie's obligations, and a direct systemic risk to the real economy that would arise out of a serious financial problem at either of these two companies. We discuss both risks in separate sections.

It is no longer a source of serious debate that the federal government bears some direct risk associated with its chartering and sponsorship of Fannie Mae and Freddie Mac. These two companies are called *government-sponsored enterprises* (hence, the acronym GSEs) because they have government charters, important links to the government, and various privileges and immunities that ordinary private companies do not enjoy.[2] In addition, they are specifically charged with a government mission: providing liquidity to the secondary market in mortgages. The government's ultimate responsibility for their financial condition is further confirmed by the fact that they are regulated and supervised for financial soundness by a government agency—something that would not be necessary if, in reality, the government bore no responsibility for them.

Moreover, although the government routinely denies any commitment or responsibility with respect to these and other GSEs—indeed, the relevant provisions of the charters of Fannie and Freddie explicitly declare that their securities are not government guaranteed—its behavior in the past has convinced the capital markets that the government will not allow either company to fail. In 1987, for example, when another government-sponsored enterprise, the Farm Credit System, became insolvent, Congress and the administration developed and implemented a $4 billion bailout plan, confirming the capital markets' view about what the government would do if Fannie and Freddie were to experience financial difficulty.

At the end of 2003, Fannie and Freddie had incurred obligations of almost $4 trillion, consisting of direct borrowing of $1.8 trillion and guarantees of mortgage-backed securities (MBSs) of more than $1.9 trillion.[3] A loss of even a small portion of this sum, requiring the federal government to step in, would dwarf the losses in the savings and loan (S&L) debacle of the late 1980s and early 1990s. Losses of a substantial size, requiring some form of government intervention, are not entirely out of the question. The housing GSEs are highly leveraged, far more so than banks or other financial institutions of equivalent size. Table A-1 (appendix 1) is a table prepared by the Office of Management and Budget that compares the capital positions of the housing GSEs to the capital positions of other major U.S. financial institutions.

Moreover, because of their government backing, Fannie and Freddie face little market discipline. Investors, believing that the government will not permit Fannie or Freddie to fail, readily provide funds at rates that are not commensurate with the risks these companies would represent without their government support. Thus, Fannie and Freddie are able to expand indefinitely, held in check only by the minimal capital requirements—2.5 percent for on-balance-sheet obligations and 45 basis points for off-balance-sheet obligations—statutorily required by their charters.

As Fed Chairman Alan Greenspan noted in testimony to the Senate Banking Committee on February 24, 2004,

> As a general matter, we rely in a market economy upon market discipline to constrain the leverage of firms, including financial institutions. However, the existence, or even the perception, of government backing undermines the effectiveness of market discipline. A market system relies on the vigilance of lenders and investors in market transactions to assure themselves of their

counterparties' strength. However, many counterparties in GSE transactions, when assessing their risk, clearly rely instead on the GSEs' perceived special relationship to the government. Thus, with housing-related GSEs, regulators cannot rely significantly on market discipline. Indeed, they must assess whether these institutions hold appropriate amounts of capital relative to the risks they assume and the costs that they might impose on others, including taxpayers, in the event of a financial-market meltdown.[4]

In a speech at AEI on February 6, 2004, the chairman of Fannie Mae, Franklin Raines, argued that, despite its leverage, Fannie does not represent a significant risk to the government or the taxpayers because it is invested in home mortgages, one of the safest investments in the world.[5] This argument may be accurate with respect to credit risk, but it ignores completely the real risks—interest rate and prepayment risk—that Fannie and Freddie incur when they borrow funds to purchase mortgages and MBSs for their portfolios. Since these borrowings amount to approximately $1.8 trillion, this is a risk that cannot be ignored or swept under the rug with references to the relative safety of investing in mortgages.

Mortgages and MBSs, although highly creditworthy in themselves, are among the most risky of investments from the standpoint of interest rate risk. This is because U.S. homeowners have the option to refinance their mortgages when interest rates decline. In that case, Fannie and Freddie may be left with liabilities that are more costly than the yield on the replacement mortgages they subsequently acquire. On the other hand, if interest rates rise, homeowners generally will not refinance, and Fannie and Freddie may be required to refinance their debt at rates that exceed the yield on their mortgage portfolios.

In his Senate Banking Committee testimony, Chairman Greenspan also noted:

> Interest rate risk associated with fixed-rate mortgages, unless supported by substantial capital . . . can be of even greater concern than . . . credit risk. Interest rate volatility combined with the ability of homeowners to prepay their mortgages without

penalty means that the cash flows associated with the holding of mortgage debt directly or through mortgage-backed securities are highly uncertain, even if the probability of default is low. In general, interest rate risk is readily handled by adjusting maturities of assets and liabilities. But hedging prepayment risk is more complex. To manage this risk with little capital requires a conceptually sophisticated hedging framework. In essence, the current system depends on the risk managers at Fannie and Freddie to do everything just right, rather than depending on a market-based system supported by the risk assessments and management capabilities of many participants with different views and different strategies for hedging risks. Our financial system would be more robust if we relied on a market-based system that spreads interest rate risks, rather than the current system, which concentrates such risk with the GSEs.[6]

To address these risks, Fannie and Freddie purchase various kinds of derivatives, such as interest rate swaps, but these carry risks of their own—particularly the possibility that counterparties may default precisely at the time that the protection of a derivative is necessary. What is more, none of these hedges is perfect, and achieving complete protection against interest rate risk would drastically reduce Fannie and Freddie's profitability. As a result, it is likely that both companies are taking some interest rate risk by hedging only a portion of the risk they are incurring. That Fannie at least was following this course was demonstrated in mid-2002, when the company reported a negative duration gap of fourteen months, indicating that the average maturity of its liabilities exceeded the average maturity of its assets by fourteen months. The likely reason for this is that the company was betting that interest rates would rise, and hence that its lower-cost liabilities would be a source of profit.

Fannie and Freddie are a classic example of what is known as privatizing profits but socializing risk. Ordinarily, without the government's backing, companies with the thin capitalizations and high risks of Fannie and Freddie would be unable to attract funds at a price that would enable them to acquire portfolios of mortgages or MBSs. With the government's backing, they are able to do this, but in the process they are placing the risk of loss on the taxpayers while retaining the profits for themselves. In the case of Fannie's duration gap, if interest rates had fallen steeply during the period when the maturity of Fannie's liabilities significantly exceeded the maturity of its assets, Fannie might have suffered serious losses when homeowners refinanced their mortgages to achieve lower rates. As it happened, this did not occur, but the incident showed the degree to which Fannie's management could create risks for the taxpayers without any substantial controls.

In 2003, a similar incident occurred involving Freddie. In this case, the company reported that errors had been made in its accounting and dismissed its top three corporate managers. One year later, Freddie has still not been able to issue audited financial statements for any portion of 2003. Newspaper reports indicate that Freddie's management manipulated the company's financial reports to smooth earnings and hide the degree to which the company was dependent on derivatives to manage its interest rate risk. Again, no serious harm was done, but the incident showed that the management of Freddie, like the management of Fannie, was not acting prudently.

The danger is that the next mistake by either management will not be as benign or as easily corrected. Then, the consequences for the taxpayers and the economy generally could be dire.

Systemic Risk. When economists refer to systemic risk, they are referring to the danger than an event in the financial system, such as the failure of a large depository institution, will affect the wider economy, perhaps by slowing down economic activity or causing other losses. An occurrence that has this effect, referred to as a *systemic event*, is generally produced by a shock—an unexpected adverse development—that causes investors and other market participants to reevaluate existing relationships.

Systemic risk is generally discussed in the context of depository institutions, but over the years, new requirements for minimum capital, deposit insurance, and prompt corrective action when financial weakness is developing, have reduced the likelihood that banks—even large ones—will create systemic events. However, these regulatory safeguards do not exist in the case of Fannie and Freddie. Their regulation is notoriously weak, and the implicit government backing they enjoy reduces or eliminates the market discipline that would ordinarily prevent them from taking unwise risks. As many studies have shown, their regulator, the Office of Federal Housing Enterprise Oversight (OFHEO), lacks many of the powers routinely provided the regulators of depository institutions.[7]

Moreover, Fannie and Freddie are unique entities in that they have all the attributes of financial institutions but also dominate and are central to the housing industry, a major sector of the real economy. In contrast, no depository institution, or even group of depository institutions, so dominates an important market. In addition, because of the advantages they have been granted by law, Fannie's and Freddie's debt securities are held widely and without prudential limit by banks and other financial institutions. In many cases, especially among small banks, Fannie's and Freddie's securities constitute more that 100 percent of their capital.[8]

These two elements, unique among financial institutions, make financial problems at Fannie or Freddie far more likely to trigger a systemic event than similar problems at other financial institutions of comparable size. Assuming that a potential systemic event occurs, it will be transmitted directly to the housing market and from there to the wider economy. It will also immediately weaken the financial condition of banks and other financial institutions that hold the debt securities of Fannie and Freddie, reducing their ability to lend.

How could a systemic event come about? A February 2003 report by OFHEO[9] (OFHEO Report) outlines several scenarios where severe financial problems at Fannie or Freddie could become systemic events. The worst-case scenario describes a set of facts that does not seem so remote, given that we now know of severe deficiencies in the accounting and financial reporting at Freddie. These were unknown to the financial markets until the company changed its auditors and was required to file financial reports with the SEC for the first time. Freddie's problems were so severe that it fell seriously behind in issuing periodic financial statements. Fortunately, the nature of the deficiencies, which involved understating its earnings, did not alarm the markets when disclosed. The reaction might not be the same if one of the two companies were suddenly to report serious and unanticipated losses.

In any event, the OFHEO Report scenario unfolds as follows: "Enterprise A unexpectedly incurs large losses. . . . Investors generally do not believe Enterprise A is viable and are uncertain about whether it will default, about the size of any credit losses they may incur, and about the future liquidity of its debt. That uncertainty leads to widespread selling of Enterprise A's debt as well as a large decline in the market prices of its MBS." The scenario points out that, under some circumstances, Enterprise B might be able to pick up A's business, so the housing finance system would continue with slightly higher mortgage rates. However, "if Enterprise B cannot expand its activities quickly, a significant short-term decline in mortgage lending, home sales, and housing starts occurs, contributing to problems elsewhere in the economy and increasing the likelihood of macroeconomic losses." In some circumstances, the report continues, "the sell-off of Enterprise A's debt becomes a panic, so that trading in those obligations virtually ceases, at least for a time. . . . Illiquidity in the market for Enterprise A's debt and the plunge in the market value of its MBS exacerbate liquidity problems at many banks and thrifts."[10]

This scenario might be remote; it might not. But it points out that a sudden shock at Fannie and Freddie is not the same as a sudden shock at an ordinary bank, even a large one. The systemic danger from a bank's failure is its connections to other financial institutions, particularly other banks. If a bank cannot meet its obligations, other banks might also be unable to meet theirs. In this way, a shock at a large bank can spread through the financial system and cause losses in the real economy as economic activity slows or stops while the crisis continues.

However, a shock at Fannie or Freddie will move differently through the economy. If either is unable to function, the housing market could be directly and immediately affected: Mortgage rates could rise, financing of housing could slow, housing starts could decline, and all the other industries in the U.S. economy that depend on housing (furniture, appliances, and construction, among many others) could be adversely affected. Moreover, if the value of Fannie's or Freddie's debt securities falls, large numbers of banks will have impaired capital, at least on a marked-to-market basis, and may reduce or stop lending until their capital position improves. This would add a further depressing effect on economic activity.

Therefore, because of their dominance in the housing market and the importance of that market to the U.S. economy as a whole, a serious financial problem at Fannie or Freddie would be far worse than a similar problem at even the largest banks. In the case of a big-bank meltdown, the Fed can always provide additional liquidity to the market, so as to alleviate concern about the availability of funds, but the Fed cannot provide a lifeline for a housing finance system that depends for its functioning on only two companies, and cannot restore the capital of the thousands of banks that held large amounts of Fannie and Freddie debt.[11] That can be done only by Congress, which will have to rescue Fannie or Freddie, or both, with taxpayer funds.

Can a GSE produce a systemic event? This brings us to an important question: If, in fact, Fannie and Freddie are implicitly backed by the U.S. government, why should there be any systemic event arising out of a financial shock? Indeed, in the early 1980s, Fannie Mae was insolvent for an extended period and still able to obtain funding in the capital markets.

For a number of reasons, Fannie Mae did not face adverse financial market conditions when it became insolvent more than twenty years ago. At the time, the insolvency of large numbers of S&Ls was well known in the markets. Congress had made clear through a congressional resolution in March 1982 that the full faith and credit of the United States stood behind the deposit insurance funds and it would take whatever steps were necessary to assure stability in the housing finance market. Fannie Mae's condition was no surprise, as it was part of the same syndrome—high interest rates—that had caused the S&L industry to become insolvent. The problems of the S&L industry and Fannie Mae were thus seen as temporary: something that would rectify itself when interest rates declined. Finally, Fannie Mae was considerably smaller than it is today, even in relation to the smaller size of the government at that time. There was little doubt in the markets that the government could bail out Fannie Mae, if necessary, without creating a heavy cost to taxpayers.

If an event with systemic potential should occur today, circumstances would be very different. First, it will be a surprise. Because of the weak supervision and lack of transparency at Fannie and Freddie, a serious financial reverse is likely to be a shock to the markets. The markets today are globalized, including many foreign financial institutions and central banks that are large holders of Fannie and Freddie debt. These holders, not fully understanding U.S. politics, will be inclined to dump their securities first and ask questions afterward, driving down prices and possibly causing panic selling among U.S. investors, too. Congress, which alone would have the authority to close the failing institution or provide the financing to sustain it, might not be in session, or if it is, there could be debate about whether the taxpayers should assume all the losses or share some with the creditors. Since Fannie and Freddie have over $3 trillion in obligations outstanding, the question is not without significance or political cost.

Moreover, as noted in the OFHEO Report, "Today, financial information is disseminated much more rapidly, and investors rebalance their portfolios in response to much smaller changes in financial market conditions and economic indicators. Those changes and aspects of the government's relationship to the Enterprises [Fannie and Freddie] suggest that it would be possible for the market for the debt of an Enterprise that had serious solvency problems to become illiquid."[12]

Accordingly, in the context of an event with systemic potential, little comfort can be taken from the fact that Fannie and Freddie enjoy implicit government support. That support will almost certainly come at some point, but the delays and uncertainties associated with who, if anyone, will actually share losses with U.S. taxpayers could mean that a great deal of damage will be done to the U.S. economy while these questions are resolved.

Mission Creep. Although not strictly a financial risk, mission creep represents a serious danger to the U.S. financial system. Initially chartered to provide liquidity to the residential mortgage market, Fannie and Freddie have made, and continue to make, forays into other areas of the financial economy. These include:

1. Expanding purchases of home equity loans. Although justified as providing funds for home improvement, these loans (many of which are cash-out refinances) are used primarily for general consumer or household purposes or for debt consolidation, and are thus consumer lending.

2. Expansion into the sales of residential real estate beyond the properties they have acquired through foreclosure. Freddie has

purchased a real estate owned (REO) disposition company, which offers this service to other lenders. Complaints to the U.S. Department of Housing and Urban Development (HUD) about this acquisition have drawn no response.

3. Making their automated underwriting systems accessible to realtors and consumers, so that it will be possible to determine in advance whether a loan to a potential homebuyer will qualify for purchase by one of the GSEs. In this way, the GSEs will be able to create a "portable" mortgage approval, allowing realtors and consumers to cut out mortgage lenders, who will no longer have an underwriting role in the transaction.

4. Lending to the developers of apartment housing, including luxury apartments. In doing this, Fannie and Freddie use resources that could be used to expand home ownership, compete with home ownership as a housing goal, and engage in what is essentially commercial real estate lending. In 2003, Fannie received approval from HUD to offer construction and development loans.

5. In an alliance with Countrywide Credit, Fannie will market appraisal services, title insurance, floodplain determination, and full-service insurance agency and mutual fund management. Although Fannie will not perform these services itself, it is using its power in the housing market to favor certain providers of housing-related services. This will reduce competition and further concentrate these industries. In addition, Freddie Mac has combined its database with that of an electronic appraisal firm to provide electronic appraisal services in competition with others in the field.

6. Fannie Mae's long-term plans clearly involve pushing into consumer lending. In a speech to the investment community in 1999, Fannie Chairman Franklin D. Raines stated:

> Another way we are going to expand the mortgage debt market is to help consumers capitalize on the equity in their homes *for things they need*, whether it's reverse mortgages to

> finance retirement, or home equity loans to expand or improve their homes. For example, we have a pilot with Home Depot stores and some of our lenders where consumers can apply for home improvement loans right in the stores. The demographics for these mortgage products are terrific as Baby Boom families grow and retire. This will move some of the equity side of the $12 trillion housing market onto the debt side. [emphasis added][13]

Needless to say, retiring baby boomers will not be using reverse mortgages and the like to fix up their homes.

Because of their government backing, Fannie and Freddie are able to underprice any other lender. This has given them an unassailable oligopsony (only two buyers) and dominance of the residential real estate finance market. There are serious problems with this state of affairs, as in any case where a substantial portion of any important market is controlled by only two companies. Such markets are characterized by limited competition, higher prices, and a lack of innovation. This is probably true of the residential mortgage market in the United States, but because of the absence of comparable markets, it is difficult to demonstrate.

It can be argued, of course, that, in chartering Fannie and Freddie and giving them implicit government backing, Congress intended, for whatever reason, to create this outcome. However, it is highly unlikely that Congress intended to allow these two companies to enter—let alone dominate—other areas of the financial economy. Yet, looking at the preceding list, it is clear that Fannie and Freddie are beginning to move into consumer and commercial lending as well as activities in the residential real estate market related to the home-buying process.

This expansion is necessary if Fannie and Freddie are to continue to grow in revenue and profitability. The fact is that they have now grown so large that they are beginning to run out of mortgages to buy and hold or securitize. Although current numbers are hard to find because of Freddie's inability to file financial reports with the SEC, it is likely that Fannie and Freddie together hold in portfolio or have guaranteed, through mortgage-backed securities, more than 75 percent of all conventional and conforming mortgages in the United States. At some point, as they continue to expand faster than the mortgage market itself, they will find themselves unable to continue growing, their stock price will fall, and they will enter a period of retrenchment. To avoid this, they are proceeding on several fronts. Through supporters in Congress, they are attempting to raise the conforming loan limit, so that they can extend their activities deeper in the so-called jumbo market. In addition, as noted, they are expanding horizontally into commercial and consumer lending and vertically into home-buying services such as appraisal and title insurance.[14]

The danger here is that Fannie and Freddie will be able to use their government backing to take over additional markets, causing concentration where there is now competition, and stifling innovation. This is not the same danger as financial or systemic risk, but over the long term it could prove more harmful to the U.S. economy than either of these.

Can Regulation Substantially Reduce These Risks?

The current view in Congress is that Fannie and Freddie must be more effectively regulated and, if legislation is adopted granting greater regulatory authority to some entity, whether a part of the Treasury or an independent commission, the risks these two companies represent will be significantly reduced. This might indeed be true if Fannie and Freddie were ordinary companies, but they are not. Together they are among the most politically powerful entities in Washington, backed by support from the industries that benefit from their activities: home builders, realtors, mortgage bankers, and securities underwriters. Moreover, their extensive advertising has created the false impression that they are essential to the provision of affordable housing to disadvantaged groups. As many studies have shown, however, they lag ordinary banks in this respect.

But the political power that Fannie and Freddie can muster changes significantly the ability of a government regulator to reduce the risks they create through their operations. For example, if the regulator should decide that, in the interests of their safety and soundness—and the protection of taxpayers—their capital should be increased, the outcry would be deafening. Fannie and Freddie will argue that increasing their capital requirements will make mortgages more expensive or reduce their availability, and this argument will be backed by their constituent groups. There will be calls and messages to Congress about the damage this will do to home ownership or the economy generally, and Congress will respond with calls and messages to the regulator—all these bearing a single concise message: back off. Under these circumstances, it will be very difficult for a regulator—any regulator—to take steps that would have these supposedly dire effects when it is acting only to prevent some theoretical danger somewhere in the future.

The same thing would be true if the regulator were to attempt to confine Fannie and Freddie to the secondary mortgage market, preventing them from continuing their horizontal and vertical expansion. Again, the regulator would likely be compelled to back away from a direct confrontation with Fannie and Freddie and their powerful constituency groups.

As it happens, we have a recent example of how this occurs. In the late 1980s, it had become clear that the S&L industry was not recovering along with the economy. Many S&Ls were insolvent, kept open only by regulatory forbearance and the fact that deposit insurance enabled them to raise funds despite their ill health. However, efforts to close down S&Ls were resisted by the industry, and few in Congress were willing to insist that this action be taken or provide the funds necessary for an industry cleanup. Because of delays, the problem became worse and worse, as S&Ls, "gambling for resurrection," made risky bets with government-insured funds in the hope of recovering their lost capital.

The S&Ls, although a powerful industry, were not remotely as powerful as Fannie and Freddie are today. Yet they were able to stall necessary regulatory action for years while losses multiplied. This history should be a lesson for those who believe that the risks created by Fannie and Freddie can be easily contained through tighter regulation and a change in their regulator. We still live in a political system where political imperatives can trump substance, and no one should be confident that, when the time comes for a regulator to take steps adverse to Fannie and Freddie's interest, the political context will favor or even permit this action.

Recently, members of Congress—including the ranking Democrat on the House Financial Services Committee—have been complaining that proposed prudential regulation of Fannie and Freddie is too tough, and Republicans have been complaining that HUD regulations intended to increase Fannie's and Freddie's assistance to affordable and low-income housing are too ambitious. This is only a foretaste of what will occur if a regulator actually tries to rein them in.

Finally, there are limits to what a regulator can know. The major decisions of regulated companies—the ones that can be the source of financial crises—are not voluntarily disclosed to regulators. An example of this was the 2003 disclosure by Freddie Mac that its top three officers had been responsible for manipulating its financial reports. OFHEO, Freddie's regulator (which had claimed that it had good information on Fannie and Freddie and engaged in continuous monitoring), was apparently informed of this matter only the day before the three officers were dismissed.

It is important to recognize that, as long as Fannie and Freddie are perceived as government backed, they will continue to pose a serious systemic risk. Regulation will not be a satisfactory solution. As Alan Greenspan noted in the testimony cited previously,

> World-class regulation, by itself, may not be sufficient and indeed, as suggested by Treasury Secretary Snow, may even worsen the situation if the market participants infer from such regulation that the government is all the more likely to back GSE debt. This is the heart of a dilemma in designing regulation for the GSEs. On the one hand, if the regulation of the GSEs is strengthened, the market may view them even more as extensions of the government and view their debt as government debt. The result, short of a marked increase in capital, would be to expand the implicit subsidy and allow the GSEs to play an even larger unconstrained role in the financial markets. On the other hand, if we fail to strengthen GSE regulation, the possibility of an actual crisis or insolvency is increased.[15]

It takes little interpretive skill to recognize the implications of Chairman Greenspan's statement: that the only viable solution to the risks posed by Fannie and Freddie is privatization, removing them entirely from the government's account, placing them in direct competition with other financial institutions, and subjecting them to market discipline. In the balance of this paper, we present a plan for privatization that will not only accomplish these things without disrupting the residential mortgage markets but also offer the prospect of a more-efficient, lower-cost system for financing home mortgages.

In the Privatization Act, we do not propose any particular structure or agency for the regulation of Fannie and Freddie and the Federal Home Loan Banks. Although how these GSEs are regulated is important, it is not the focus of the act, and if the act is adopted, regulation of the GSEs would be required for only a five-year period until they are finally sunsetted. Nevertheless, we believe that the best regulator and supervisor during this limited period would be the Treasury Department, which alone has the political clout and financial expertise to steer what will be a turbulent course to privatization.

Do Fannie and Freddie Deliver Benefits Worth These Risks?

Given all the risks they create for taxpayers and the economy generally and the fact that their political power makes it unlikely that regulation can be effective to reduce these risks, the question still remains whether Fannie and Freddie deliver benefits to the housing economy that outweigh these considerations. Here, the answer is clearly no. Numerous studies have shown that the sole benefit that Fannie and Freddie deliver to the market is a reduction in interest rates of about 25 basis points (one-quarter of 1 percent) for conventional/conforming loans. To put this in context, every time the Federal Reserve Board raises or lowers interest rates by ¼ point as part of its monetary policy responsibilities, it has potentially the same effect on the ability of homeowners to afford a home as the combined resources and activities of Fannie Mae and Freddie Mac. Moreover, many economists believe that the reduction in rates effected by Fannie and Freddie—a result of passing through a portion of the benefits they receive from their government backing—may be of more assistance to home sellers than home buyers. Their argument is that the lower interest rates allow the sellers of homes to raise their prices.

At an AEI conference on October 25, 2002, Joseph McKenzie of the Federal Housing Finance Board presented a table that summarized most of the major studies that have attempted to estimate the effect of Fannie and Freddie in lowering interest rates for conventional and conforming loans. The table is reproduced as appendix 2. Similarly, in 2001, the Congressional Budget Office estimated that in 2000 Fannie and Freddie received a subsidy equal to 41 basis points for each mortgage, of which it passed along 25 basis points to the home buyer and retained 16 basis points for themselves.[16]

Since this conference, in an influential paper, Wayne Passmore of the Federal Reserve Board staff has estimated that Fannie and Freddie, despite their government backing, account for only a 7-basis-point reduction in the interest rates paid by homeowners on their mortgages.[17]

Finally, although supporters and officials of Fannie and Freddie frequently argue that their implicit government backing enhances mortgage market stability, this at best is a matter of chance. An example often cited is the GSEs' purchase of MBSs and mortgages in 1998 when international financial markets were disrupted by a Russian default and other factors. Thus, in a 2003 paper sponsored by Fannie Mae, economist David Gross argued that an implicit guarantee was a benefit to mortgage market stability:

> In 1998, during the period of international currency crises abroad, most interest rate spreads between riskier and safer debt widened because of the market perception of increased aggregate risk. . . . However, while spreads between mortgage rates and Fannie Mae debt also widened, the activities of Fannie Mae and Freddie Mac helped to limit the reduction in liquidity for mortgage related assets. . . . When spreads widen, the GSEs' cost of funds is low relative to the return on mortgage assets. . . . Hence it is in their interest to purchase mortgage assets, which in turn helps return the spread to an equilibrium level. . . . By acting to maximize profits, Fannie Mae and Freddie Mac help to stabilize the mortgage market thereby insulating consumers from many bond market fluctuations.[18]

It is an attractive argument: Fannie Mae and Freddie Mac as the Invisible Hands, reaching out to protect mortgage rates and market stability by maximizing profit. However, what happens when interest trends are not so favorable? Do Fannie and Freddie continue buying mortgages when their spreads are not so wide? The answer is no. At the end of 2003 and the beginning of 2004, a four-month period, Fannie and Freddie cut back substantially on their purchase of mortgages and the size of their portfolios declined. As explained by Fannie's vice president of investor relations, "We look at mortgage-to-debt spreads. We're not going to buy a long-term asset unless it [provides] a good rate of return for us."

In other words, Fannie adds liquidity to the market—and thus narrows spreads between mortgage rates and Treasury rates—only when it is profitable to do so but not when its own spreads are unfavorable in relation to the yield it can obtain on mortgages. If this is the benefit Fannie and Freddie provide the mortgage market, it is not worth the cost. Indeed, it adds volatility rather than stability, because it suggests that mortgage interest rates depend on the relative spread between what Fannie and Freddie are required to pay for their funds and what mortgages are yielding at that time, rather than the more stable relationship between mortgage yields and money market rates generally.

Thus, Fannie and Freddie deliver very little value to the mortgage markets. Weighed against the risks they create for the taxpayers and the economy generally, there should be no question that the nation would be better off with the termination of their government backing.

Federal Home Loan Banks

Like Fannie and Freddie, the Federal Home Loan Banks gain an advantage over fully private sources of credit because of implied backing by the United States government. Originally a source of financing for the S&L industry, and thus another part of the national policy of encouraging home ownership, the FHLB system lost its reason for existence after the S&L debacle of the late 1980s and early 1990s. At that point, it had become clear that S&Ls and other depository institutions could raise funds in a national market, without the need for a government-backed funding mechanism. In addition, Congress changed the conditions for membership in the system to include banks and other institutions that were not solely devoted to making housing loans. So the FHLBs became simply a mechanism for providing preferential funding to depository institutions that chose to use the system's services and gain the benefits of government-backed funding. Needless to say, other than Congress's traditional reluctance to terminate any existing agency of government, there is no compelling policy reason for continuing the FHLB system.

The FHLB system provides few benefits to homeowners. According to the Congressional Budget Office (CBO), the FHLBs received $2.8 billion in subsidies in 2000 as a result of their implicit government backing. With this, the CBO estimated that the FHLBs reduced jumbo mortgage interest rates by 3 basis points.[19] The one apparent benefit to the economy is the development by the Federal Home Loan Bank of Chicago of the Mortgage Partnership Finance (MPF) program, which over time could provide some competition for Fannie and Freddie. MPF is in fact one reason to privatize the FHLBs at the same time that Fannie and Freddie are privatized. If Fannie and Fred-die alone are privatized, the MPF program will simply grow into the next government-backed-mortgage finance system, although none is necessary.

Although the FHLBs do not present great risks to the taxpayers and the economy, and certainly not of the same magnitude as Fannie and Freddie, they are not wholly without risk either. In the Analytical Perspectives section of the administration's 2005 budget, the Office of Management and Budget (OMB) took note of the poor financial condition of some of the FHLBs: "The Federal Home Loan Bank System . . . suffered a significant decline in profits in 2003, primarily stemming from investment losses and a failure to hedge interest rate risk adequately at several Federal Home Loan Banks. As a result, one rating organization downgraded its outlook for some individual banks of the 12-Bank system."[20]

What seems clear is that, although the FHLBs create no great risks for the taxpayers or the economy, neither do they serve any useful purpose. They receive a substantial subsidy but provide little assistance to homeowners. As the OMB noted, some of the FHLB banks have not been well managed, and because of a perception that they are backed by the government they receive little market discipline to control their risks. At some time in the future, mismanagement may be sufficiently severe to require the government to step in with financial support. If the FHLBs could point to some clear benefit they provide, this risk of future losses might be tolerable, but given that the Federal Home Loan Bank system no longer has any reason for being, it should be privatized along with Fannie and Freddie.

Affordable Housing

Study after study has shown that Fannie Mae and Freddie Mac, despite full-throated claims about trillion-dollar commitments and the like, have failed to lead the private market in assisting the development and financing of affordable housing.[21] In a sense, this was never likely to happen, because there was always a conflict between Fannie and Freddie's ownership by private shareholders and their responsibility to carry out a government mission. This should be a lesson to lawmakers that attempting to turn shareholder-owned companies into government agencies is bound to fail. The managements of shareholder-owned companies have fiduciary duties to the shareholders that can and do conflict with the performance of a government mission.[22]

Extensive advertising by Fannie and Freddie has created the impression, especially among lawmakers, that they provide financial assistance to minority and underserved groups to enable their members to become homeowners. This is not correct. The privatization of Fannie and Freddie according to the plan proposed in this memorandum will not impair the growth of affordable or low-income housing in the United States.

However, the FHLBs are subject to a statutory requirement to contribute 10 percent of their earnings toward community development projects, and this program (which has produced about $200 million in recent years) has had some impact in advancing minority and low-income housing. If the FHLBs are privatized, these funds will no longer be available. The legislation provides for fees to be levied on Fannie and Freddie and the FHLBs if they fail to meet certain deadlines. It is impossible to know at this point whether the fees will ever be assessed, but if they are, they should be paid into an affordable housing fund.[23]

The Privatization Plan

Most plans for the privatization of Fannie Mae and Freddie Mac founder on two shoals: that the companies, when privatized, will still be so large as to be "too big to fail" and that privatization will disrupt the process of residential financing, thus harming the U.S. economy. The plan outlined in this memorandum (the Privatization Plan), developed for the American Enterprise Institute by Thomas H. Stanton, addresses both objections. The "too-big-to-fail" problem is addressed by shrinking the size of Fannie's and Freddie's asset portfolios (principally, mortgages and MBSs) as they shift their activities away from the GSE form; the problem of mortgage market disruption is addressed by continuing the securitization of mortgages and providing for a gradual transition of this activity into a non-GSE, private-sector format. In addition, the plan provides for the privatization of the FHLBs after a transition period that will prevent the sudden disruption of the FHLBs' lending services.

Privatizing Fannie Mae and Freddie Mac

Mortgages and MBSs Held in Portfolio. Immediately upon enactment of privatization legislation (the act), the plan requires Fannie Mae and Freddie Mac to stop acquiring mortgages and MBSs for their portfolios but permits them to continue their activities as GSEs solely through the securitization of mortgages and the issuance of MBSs. The immediate effect of this step will be to stop the accumulation of interest rate risk by both enterprises and simultaneously begin the process of shrinking both their portfolios and their risks.[24] However, because the process of mortgage securitization will continue, there will be no disruption of the residential mortgage market. Originators of mortgages, if they choose, will continue to sell their mortgages to Fannie and Freddie for subsequent securitization, or establish pools of mortgages against which MBSs guaranteed by Fannie or Freddie will be issued.

Since Fannie and Freddie will be forbidden to acquire any additional mortgages or MBSs for their portfolios as of the date of enactment of the act, their portfolios and their overall size will immediately begin to decline as mortgages are paid off or refinanced. To supplement this normal runoff, the plan requires that Fannie and Freddie sell off mortgages and MBSs according to a previously established five-year schedule. The purpose here is to assure that, at the end of five years from the date of enactment of the act, Fannie and Freddie will have sold off all the mortgages and MBSs they hold and will not delay disposition in the hope that Congress will eventually relieve them of this obligation. The plan contains penalties for failure to meet the required disposition schedule.

The proceeds of the sale of mortgages and MBSs will of course be used to pay down debt as it comes due during the five-year period after enactment. Nevertheless, at the end of that period, Fannie and Freddie are likely still to have outstanding debt contracted while they were GSEs. The plan provides for this debt to be defeased in a transaction in which Treasury securities in an amount sufficient to pay all interest and principal on the outstanding GSE debt will be placed in separate trusts by Fannie and Freddie. As the debt comes due, the proceeds of the sale of the Treasury securities will be used to liquidate it.

After providing for the defeasance of remaining debt, Fannie's and Freddie's charters will sunset and their remaining assets and liabilities be transferred to the holding companies they were permitted to establish, as described later. If Fannie and Freddie have taken certain necessary steps, also described later, their holding companies will be permitted to carry on any business, including the businesses of acquiring and securitizing mortgages.

Mortgage Securitization and the Issuance of MBSs. For six months after enactment, Fannie and Freddie will be permitted to continue to securitize mortgages and issue and guarantee MBSs without limit. Thereafter, for the next two and a half years, they will be required gradually to phase down their GSE securitization activities according to a schedule that will result in the complete termination of these activities three years from the date of enactment. At the end of this period, the remaining MBSs in trusts operated by Fannie and Freddie will be transferred to one or more well-capitalized trusts with independent trustees. The following summarizes the sequential privatization steps required under the plan:

Date of enactment

All purchases of mortgages and MBSs for portfolio cease.

Mortgage portfolio begins to run off.

Securitization continues as before.

Six months after date of enactment

Phase-out of GSE securitization activity begins.

10 percent of mortgage and MBSs portfolio on date of
enactment (DOE) should have been liquidated.

One year after enactment

GSE securitization activity should be reduced by 20 percent.

20 percent of DOE mortgage and MBS portfolio should
have been liquidated.

Two years after enactment

GSE securitization activity reduced by 60 percent.

40 percent of DOE mortgage and MBS portfolio should
have been liquidated.

Three years after enactment

GSE securitization terminates.

60 percent of DOE mortgage and MBS portfolio should
have been liquidated.

Four years after enactment

80 percent of DOE mortgage and MBS portfolio should have
been liquidated.

Five years after enactment

100 percent of DOE mortgage and MBS portfolio should
have been liquidated.

Remaining mortgages backing outstanding MBSs are
transferred to trusts.

Debt not yet extinguished is defeased.

Charters sunset.

The phase-down of Fannie and Freddie's securitization will not necessarily result in any diminution in the total amount of securitization activity in the market. First, if Fannie and Freddie comply with two requirements outlined later, they will be permitted to set up non-GSE affiliates, under ordinary state-chartered corporations functioning as holding companies, to continue securitizing mortgages. These companies, as will be described, can engage in any other activity permitted by the laws of the state of their chartering. Second, once Fannie and Freddie (as GSEs) no longer occupy the entire field for securitization of conventional and conforming loans, many other companies that currently securitize mortgages in the so-called jumbo market will be able to compete for product in the conventional and conforming market.

The Establishment of Holding Companies and Affiliates. Immediately after the enactment of the act, Fannie and Freddie will be permitted to establish holding companies—ordinary corporations chartered under the law of a state. These companies will be authorized to engage in any activity permissible for corporations chartered in that state and will be the parent companies of both Fannie and Freddie and their non-GSE affiliates that, among other things, will be permitted to engage in acquiring and securitizing mortgages.

However, although the various corporate steps can be taken to create these holding companies and their non-GSE subsidiaries, neither the holding companies nor any non-GSE subsidiaries will be able to engage in any business activity (other than acting as the parent companies of Fannie and Freddie) until their respective GSE subsidiaries have taken two steps: (1) achieved a level of capitalization that the then regulator of Fannie and Freddie considers equivalent to the level of capitalization a company would have to maintain for its debt to be rated AA by a recognized debt rating agency; and (2) spun off, to separate companies owned, respectively, by the shareholders of Fannie and Freddie, copies of their automated underwriting systems and copies of all information in their databases that pertain to the business of underwriting, acquiring, or securitizing mortgages. The regulator of Fannie and Freddie is required by the plan to certify that all relevant information has been spun off and Fannie and Freddie continue to maintain what would be the equivalent of an AA rating on their debt.

The purpose of requiring an AA-equivalent rating is to prevent Fannie and Freddie from using their continuing GSE status to attract capital and support their operations, while transferring most of their assets to the holding company. The purpose of requiring that they spin off copies of their automated underwriting systems is to assure that, even as privatized companies, Fannie and Freddie are unable to dominate the mortgage market through their superior data on conventional/conforming mortgages or the fact that many originators have become accustomed to working within the parameters of their automated underwriting systems. By requiring that these assets be spun off to independent companies owned by their shareholders, the plan intends to give the shareholders of Fannie and Freddie an opportunity to realize the value of these assets. The spun-off companies, which will be required to maintain their independence from the GSEs, the GSEs' holding companies, or any other participants in the mortgage market, can engage in any activity, but they will be required to license the automated underwriting systems and the databases to all comers, on essentially comparable terms.

Thus, at the conclusion of this process, Fannie and Freddie will have been liquidated and their charters revoked. However, they will be succeeded by fully private companies that can engage in any activity, including the same businesses in which Fannie and Freddie engaged as GSEs. The residential finance market, in addition, will have become considerably more competitive. Instead of two companies dominating the market and earning oligopolistic profits, many companies will compete, seeking to make what are now classified as conventional/conforming loans, to hold them as investments or securitize them. It is likely that this competition and the innovations it will spawn relatively quickly will drive mortgage costs down to a level equivalent to the level that prevailed when Fannie and Freddie dominated the market. However, in this case, the shareholders of the competing companies, and not U.S. taxpayers, will bear the risks associated with this business.

This privatization program bears a strong resemblance to that of Sallie Mae, which was implemented in the mid-1990s. Sallie Mae was also privatized through the creation of a non-GSE holding company and the gradual runoff of its GSE portfolio. As the GSE portfolio declined, the business of the holding company grew, so that, after a period of years, the holding company was operating without the restrictions applicable to a GSE.

However, there are important differences between the two structures. Sallie Mae was permitted to continue buying and selling student loans through the GSE for ten years from the date of enactment, and few controls were placed on the transfer of assets from the GSE to the holding company, so that the holding company received significant benefits, courtesy of the taxpayers. In this plan, the portfolios of mortgages and MBSs held by Fannie and Freddie are not permitted to grow and are required to meet a phase-out schedule that will result in the liquidation of the entire portfolio within five years. In addition, by requiring that the GSEs maintain an AA-equivalent rating if they want to be affiliated with operating holding companies, the plan will prevent them from transferring assets to their holding company parents until they are fully liquidated.

As it happens, we believe the mortgage market can be further improved through the establishment of mortgage holding subsidiaries for banks and other entities. That concept, developed by Bert Ely for the American Enterprise Institute, is discussed later in this monograph. At this point, however, we proceed to a discussion of the privatization of the FHLBs.

Privatizing the Federal Home Loan Banks

Termination of Activities Other Than Collateralized Lending. For privatizing the Federal Home Loan Banks, the plan adopts an approach quite similar to that used with respect to privatization of Fannie and Freddie. First, the asset powers of the FHLBs (that is, the range of their financial activities) will be limited, but they will be permitted for a period of time to continue making the safest form of their advances: those collateralized by residential mortgages. This is roughly analogous to the plan's approach to the risks created by Fannie and Freddie. There, the most risky element of their activities, the growth of their portfolios of mortgages and MBSs, was immediately terminated, but to prevent disruption of the residential mortgage market, the securitization of mortgages is permitted to continue for a six-month period before phaseout begins.

The plan permits the FHLBs to continue collateralized lending for a similar six-month period, so institutions that borrow from the FHLBs can make alternative funding arrangements. Any such collateralized loans, however, could not have a maturity later than five years from the date of enactment of the Privatization Act, and all such loans would have to be match funded, so that the debts incurred to fund permissible loans did not exceed the maturity dates of the loans.

As in the case of the acquisition of mortgages and MBSs by Fannie and Freddie, all other activities of the FHLBs would be terminated immediately under the plan, including the Mortgage Partnership Finance Program and all similar programs, acquisition of assets for investment portfolios (other than the collateralized loans discussed in the previous paragraph), offering financial guarantees, and advancing loans with maturities longer than five years from the date of enactment. The assets associated with these activities would be permitted to run off. To supplement this normal runoff, the plan requires that the FHLBs sell off their assets (other than advances) according to a previously established five-year schedule. The purpose here is to assure that, at the end of five years from the date of enactment, the FHLBs will have sold off all assets they held on the enactment date, other than advances, and will not delay disposition in the hope that Congress will eventually relieve them of this obligation. The plan contains penalties for failure to meet the required disposition schedule. At the end of the five-year period from the date of enactment, any remaining assets would be placed in trusts and defeased with Treasury securities in the same way that the obligations of Fannie and Freddie were defeased. Similarly, to the extent that the debts of the FHLBs have not been extinguished during that five-year period, they also will be defeased.

At the end of six months from the date of enactment, the FHLBs must begin to phase down their GSE collateralized lending activities according to a fixed schedule, so that, at the end of three years from the date of enactment, they will no longer be offering loans or doing any other business as GSEs.

The Establishment of Holding Companies and Affiliates. Immediately on enactment, the FHLBs will be permitted to establish holding companies, which will be ordinary corporations chartered under state law. The shareholders of each holding company will be the member banks of each FHLB, and their respective percentage share interests will be equivalent to their membership interests in the FHLB of which they were members.

As with Fannie and Freddie, the holding company of each FHLB that achieves and maintains an AA-equivalent rating, as determined by its regulator, will be permitted to engage in any business permissible under the law of the state in which it is incorporated. FHLBs and their holding companies will be permitted to merge, as long as the resulting entity maintains an AA-equivalent rating.

As the FHLBs begin to phase down their GSE lending, that lending activity can be assumed by their holding companies or its non-GSE holding company subsidiaries. In this way, like Fannie and Freddie, the FHLBs can continue to carry on a financial business, through subsidiaries or otherwise, but not in GSE form. Among other things, the holding companies could become banker's banks or another form of service subsidiary for the former members of the FHLB, now its shareholders.

At the end of five years from the date of enactment, the charters of the FHLBs will terminate. At that point all their remaining obligations (primarily long-term debt that has not been sold and guarantees of instruments that have not yet been extinguished) will be defeased by transferring all such obligations to one or more trusts along with a sufficient principal amount of Treasury securities to meet any obligations as they come due. At the termination of the trust or trusts, the remaining assets will become the property of the holding companies or, if the holding companies do not exist, will be divided among the then existing institutions that were members of the former FHLB.

Lowering Housing Finance Costs

In speaking to a conference at AEI on February 6, 2004, Fannie Mae Chairman Franklin Raines argued that government backing of Fannie Mae (he denied there is a "subsidy") was a consequence of a national policy that favors homeownership.[25] This is certainly true, but it raises two important questions:

1. Given the risks they create for taxpayers and the economy generally, do Fannie and Freddie represent a sound way for the government to assist homeowners in financing their mortgages?

2. Quite apart from a cost-benefit analysis of Fannie and Freddie, is there a better, more-efficient way to finance mortgages?

The answer to the first question, as previously discussed, is clearly no. Fannie and Freddie deliver very little benefit to homeowners, perhaps as little as the 7 basis points estimated in the Passmore paper, while creating enormous risks for the taxpayers and the economy generally. Moreover, even if one were to support the idea that the government should assist homeowners to obtain lower mortgage costs, Fannie and Freddie are a very inefficient way of achieving that purpose.

Discussing the Passmore paper in his February 24 testimony, Chairman Greenspan remarked,

> Passmore's analysis suggests that Fannie and Freddie likely lower mortgage rates less than 16 basis points, with a best estimate centering on 7 basis points. If the estimated 7 basis points is correct, the associated present value of homeowner savings is only about half the after-tax subsidy that shareholders of these GSEs are estimated to receive. Congressional Budget Office and other estimates differ, but they come to essentially the same conclusion: A substantial portion of these GSEs' implicit subsidy accrues to GSE shareholders in the form of increased dividends and stock market value. Fannie and Freddie, as you know, have disputed the conclusions of many of these studies.[26]

In other words, in Chairman Greenspan's view, Fannie and Freddie and their shareholders receive substantial benefits from government backing, while homeowners, the principal intended beneficiaries of the government's policy, received relatively little.

The second question outlined above is really the key question. Given government policy favoring homeownership and a desire on the part of the government to assist homeowners in obtaining the lowest possible mortgage rates, is there a better, more-efficient mortgage-based financing system than the secondary mortgage market system that Fannie and Freddie control?

The answer here appears to be yes. In a plan developed for AEI, Bert Ely offers a financing system based on a newly authorized and established subsidiary of mortgage originators such as banks, S&Ls, and other mortgage market participants. These subsidiaries are called Mortgage Holding Subsidiaries, or MHSs, and are established expressly for the purpose of holding the mortgages originated by the parent or its depository institution affiliates.

Ely argues that, with appropriate government policy changes, MHSs will deliver all the benefits homeowners receive from Fannie and Freddie without the need for government backing. In particular, the MHS concept provides an efficient and viable substitute for Fannie and Freddie as a vehicle for funding long-term, fixed-rate home mortgages and thus should alleviate any concern that homeowners and home buyers will be disadvantaged by the elimination of Fannie and Freddie as GSEs. The MHS plan, embodied in the legislation that accompanies this memorandum, is summarized next.

In essence, the MHS plan makes it financially feasible for mortgage originators to acquire mortgages that they will hold to maturity rather than to originate for eventual sale or securitization. The current structure of the mortgage finance market, and particularly bank capitalization policies, is tilted toward the origination of residential mortgages for sale to Fannie and Freddie—to hold in their portfolios or for eventual securitization.

Bank regulations require that banks, other insured depository institutions, and bank holding companies[27] maintain both a minimum leverage capital ratio and a minimum risk-based capital amount. Although the risk-based capital requirement favors the retention of mortgages (which have a low risk weight), the leverage ratio creates a high effective capital charge associated with holding mortgages, and thus forces depository institutions to push these assets off their balance sheets into more capital-efficient financing vehicles. As a result, banks and other depository institutions, the principal mortgage originators in the United States, plan and prepare from the outset of the mortgage lending process for the eventual sale of the mortgages they originate. Ely argues that the costs associated with originating a mortgage for sale and ultimate securitization unnecessarily increase the effective or all-in interest rate on the mortgage.

Accordingly, if Congress is really serious about reducing mortgage interest rates, it should (as provided in the attached legislation) change the relevant bank regulatory requirements to make it possible for banks and other originators to hold mortgages in portfolio. This can be done simply by exempting MHSs from all bank regulatory capital requirements that otherwise are applicable to the consolidated capital requirements of a depository institution. Although in some circumstances this could be deemed to present a risk to the capital of the parent institution, the plan contemplates that the depository institution's investment in an MHS will be fully deducted from the institution's capital, so that it presents no risk to the capital position of its parent institution. Moreover, MHSs will not be permitted to accept deposits and thus will be funded entirely in the capital markets, eliminating any other rationale for applying banklike regulations. The MHS plan assumes that most MHSs will seek to achieve and maintain an AA rating, which would require an equity capital ratio of approximately 1 percent for credit risks assumed, more than double the GSEs' statutory requirement of 0.45 percent (45 basis points) for credit risks.

Because relief from the leverage requirement will make it financially feasible for an MHS to hold a mortgage to maturity, many costs associated with originating and refinancing mortgages in the course of the mortgage securitization process can be reduced or eliminated. These cost savings, in turn, would enable an MHS to offer mortgage financing for homeowners at "all-in" interest rates as low as, or lower than, those of Fannie and Freddie—and certainly even lower in the case of refinancing—all without any government backing or taxpayer risk. An all-in interest rate includes, in addition to the stated interest rate on the mortgage, the amortization of the mortgage origination costs paid by a borrower over the effective life of the mortgage (i.e., until it is paid off or refinanced). Although almost always overlooked, origination costs, as described below, raise the all-in rate quite significantly—occasionally 50 basis points or more—when a mortgage is refinanced every few years.

Cost Reductions Attributable to the Use of the MHS Vehicle. The cost argument underlying the MHS plan begins by separating the two aspects of cost associated with a mortgage: the cost of the funds to be lent and the cost of making and servicing a mortgage loan.

Financing costs. The plan assumes that an MHS will likely fund its mortgage portfolio "in situ"; that is, the purchaser of MHS debt will acquire a security interest in a specific pool of mortgages held in the portfolio of the MHS. The MHS will guarantee the yield on the pool, but the interest and prepayment risk will be borne entirely by the investor. The in-situ financing structure equalizes the financing methods of the MHS and the GSEs, since in both cases the sponsor of the pool (the MHS or one of the two GSEs) bears only credit risk.

Once the credit risks borne by an MHS and a GSE are separated out and thus equalized, it becomes clear that Fannie and Freddie have a funding cost advantage of approximately 20 basis points over an MHS rated AA. Figures A-1 through A-4, appendix 3, show the spread between an industrial credit rated AA and the funding costs of Fannie and Freddie for loan maturities of three, five, seven, and ten years.[28] This cost advantage is largely, if not entirely, the result of the GSEs' implicit government backing. In effect, this 20 basis point differential is the gap that the MHS must close in order to offer a mortgage that bears the same or a better all-in interest rate than those offered by Fannie and Freddie.

Transaction costs. The MHS plan eliminates this gap by reducing the costs of making and servicing mortgage loans. These costs include marketing, loan origination, loan servicing, credit losses, and the cost of the mortgage lender's equity capital. First, however, it is necessary to note that certain intangible costs (the taxpayer and systemic risks associated with the GSEs) are eliminated by the MHS structure, although not priced in this analysis. These are very significant costs that would be worth eliminating even if the MHS structure did not provide a mechanism for reducing the all-in interest rate on many mortgages to or below the rate on mortgages securitized through Fannie- and Freddie-guaranteed MBSs.

Origination costs. The MHS concept will reduce loan origination costs because parent banks and other mortgage lenders will originate mortgages to hold in their MHSs rather than to sell in the secondary mortgage market. Origination costs are the cash costs a borrower incurs at the time he or she obtains a new mortgage or refinances an existing mortgage. These costs include an appraisal, title insurance, flood certification, termite inspection, application fee, credit reports, mortgage broker fees, government fees and taxes, closing and settlement costs, courier charges, and miscellaneous expenses related to obtaining a mortgage. The borrower has to pay cash for these costs or they are deducted from the mortgage proceeds, which effectively means they are financed at the mortgage rate of interest over the life of the mortgage.

Many costs in the origination process can be reduced or eliminated if the mortgage originator never intends to sell the mortgage to an unrelated party in the secondary mortgage market. Origination costs vary greatly, depending on house price, mortgage amount, jurisdiction where the home is located, and how well the costs are identified and quantified. For example, Fannie Mae estimated that origination costs ranged from $1,601 to $2,144 where a mortgage was originated through a correspondent and estimated that origination costs ranged from $1,524 when the underwriting process was highly automated to $2,549 when manual underwriting was used.[29] In 2003, the *Washington Post* cited closing costs ranging from $1,207 in North Carolina to $3,001 in Florida, with a $1,834 average for Maryland, a $1,924 average for Virginia, and a $1,957 average for Washington, D.C.[30]

The savings on origination costs could be substantial, as shown by the following example. Let us assume that a purchase mortgage of $100,000, carrying an 8 percent interest rate, is refinanced every three years (as could well have been the case over the last decade) and that the home is sold at the end of the twelfth year, triggering a mortgage payoff. Further assume the mortgage was refinanced at the progressively lower rates of 7, 6, and finally 5.5 percent. Finally, assume an initial mortgage origination cost of $1,000 and a $500 charge for each refinance. This reduction in origination costs, from $1,500 per origination or refinance, spread over twelve years, reduces the all-in mortgage interest rate by 31 basis points, *exceeding in itself* the interest rate benefit Fannie and Freddie deliver to homeowners. That is, even though, on the basis of funding costs alone, a mortgage funded by Fannie- or Freddie-guaranteed MBSs could be 20 basis points lower than a mortgage that could be delivered by any other source, that rate savings is more than offset by the higher cost, over the effective life of the mortgage, of originating and periodically refinancing that mortgage through secondary market securitization.

The cost savings, in basis points, for larger mortgages is not as great, because origination costs are lower in relation to the size of the mortgage, but the savings are still significant. For example, assuming a $200,000 mortgage with the same refinancing frequency and interest rates just set out (except for a $2,000 initial origination cost), the reduction in the all-in rate of interest would equal about 22 basis points over the life of the loan. This second example highlights a key advantage of the MHS concept: The benefits, in terms of interest-rate reduction, will be proportionally greater for smaller mortgages, which tend to be taken out by lower-income families purchasing inexpensive homes. This feature should enhance the attractiveness of the MHS concept for those who believe lower mortgages rates are key to expanding homeownership opportunities.

Servicing costs. Where mortgages are securitized, mortgage-servicing rights are accounted for as an asset by the mortgage originator and often sold later for hedging purposes; there is an active market for servicing rights. However, an originator that keeps the mortgages it originates by selling them to its MHS will not, under present accounting rules, create any servicing right to sell, and so will not incur any expense in preparing them for sale. Further, mortgage originators will lower their servicing expenses by originating mortgages to meet their own servicing standards, not industry standards governing the sale of mortgage servicing rights, which may require additional costs. Thus, in addition to trimming origination costs, the MHS structure should reduce servicing costs by a few basis points per mortgage dollar outstanding by (1) not requiring the originator to prepare to sell servicing rights; (2) not requiring the originator to account for servicing rights as an asset and to hedge those rights for prepayment risk; (3) permitting the issuer to integrate mortgage servicing more closely with other services provided to the homeowner; (4) reducing credit risk costs because of a broader customer relationship; and (5) increasing cross-selling opportunities, particularly for property-related services such as property insurance, home equity lines of credit, owners' title insurance, and credit life insurance.

If the bank can retain the ownership of the mortgage in its MHS, it is also more likely that homeowners will finance and refinance their mortgages where they have their primary banking relationship, This would allow the bank or thrift to capture the synergies of an integrated customer relationship, an element that will also result in a lower mortgage interest rate.

Together, the estimated savings to the borrower could reach 5 basis points, or one-half the present average estimated cost of mortgage servicing. No estimate has been made of the value of the other benefits of this closer, more-integrated customer relationship; but in a recent study of the European mortgage market, the author noted that "there is strong evidence from interviews with mortgage lenders that the mortgage product is increasingly being seen as a 'gateway' product to gain access to the customer and use as a basis for cross-selling other products."[31]

Competition among MHSs in selling their in-situ financing securities will force an optimal level of transparency in mortgages financed with in-situ securities, specifically with regard to prepayment characteristics. If the non-GSE mortgage-backed securities marketplace (the so-called jumbo market) is any guide, the transparency of in-situ financing will be far greater than the transparency of GSE MBS. In-situ financing investors will pay for that transparency by demanding a lower yield premium than they now demand on GSE MBSs; that is, there will be a reduction in the basis points investors demand for assuming uncertainty.

In addition, greater transparency will reduce the cross-subsidy now flowing from mortgages that prepay slowly to mortgages that prepay quickly. This cross-subsidy, which flows from the less well off to the better off, arises because the prepayment option in fixed-rate mortgages provides a benefit only when it is exercised; those who refinance more frequently tend to be higher-income, more-sophisticated borrowers. MBS investors value more highly, and therefore will accept a lower yield on, mortgage pools with slower prepayment characteristics. Greater transparency in MHS "in-situ" securitizations should reduce this cross-subsidy, which will benefit lower-income homeowners.

By using the in-situ technique to finance mortgages originated by their parent banks, large MHSs should be able to construct mortgage pools with larger tranches of securities than is true of many GSE MBS tranches. This will make in-situ securities more liquid, which in turn should further reduce interest rates on home mortgages as marketplace competition pushes the benefits of greater liquidity through to borrowers, in the form of lower mortgage rates. A firm estimate has not been developed for this potential cost savings, but a savings of even a few basis points per mortgage dollar financed would be significant, since each basis point of cost savings

Examples of MHS Interest-Rate Savings

Cost Savings (basis points per mortgage dollar)	Mortgage Amount	
	$100,000	$200,000
Origination	31	22
Servicing	5	5
Greater transparency	5	5
Larger financing tranches	2	2
Total savings	43	34
GSE funding advantage	(20)	(20)
Net savings for borrowers	23	14

Source: Author's calculations.

in the $5.7 billion home mortgage market equals approximately $570 million annually.[32]

The estimated cost savings associated with the MHS vehicle, discussed previously, are summarized in the following table, using two different mortgage amounts. In both cases, the total savings exceed the funding cost advantage Fannie and Freddie enjoy as a result of their implicit government backing.

This discussion summarized numerous cost benefits of the MHS concept relative to MBS financing by Fannie and Freddie. If the MHS structure is not burdened with unnecessary costs associated with bank capital requirements, we have demonstrated that the lower mortgage origination and servicing costs for mortgages financed through the MHS structure can overcome the 20 basis point funding cost advantage Fannie and Freddie enjoy because of their implicit government backing. The other efficiencies cited—marketing synergies, greater transparency for investors, particularly with regard to prepayment risk—should provide additional cost savings that intense marketplace competition will force through to home buyers. Finally, the elimination of the intangible costs associated with the taxpayer and systemic risks created by Fannie and Freddie alone justify adopting a mortgage financing system that does not depend on government support.

Section-by-Section Summary:
The Federal Housing Enterprises Privatization Act

Thomas H. Stanton

Section 1. Short title and table of contents

TITLE I—IMPROVEMENT OF SUPERVISION; DEFINITIONS

Section 101. Supervision

Provides that the regulator of the three housing GSEs shall have all necessary authority to discharge the responsibilities assigned by this Act, including general regulatory authority, and shall use all supervisory and enforcement authority available under existing law to assure that the purposes of this Act are carried out.

Section 102. Definitions

Defines terms used in this Act. The term "enterprise" means Fannie Mae or Freddie Mac, "Bank" means a Federal Home Loan Bank, "System" means the Federal Home Loan Bank System, etc.

TITLE II—TERMINATION OF CERTAIN ACTIVITIES
OF FANNIE MAE AND FREDDIE MAC

Section 201. Restrictions on new activities and acquisition of assets

Freezes loan limits on the enactment date; prohibits the enterprises from engaging in new business activities and from acquiring new assets except that the enterprises may (1) issue mortgage-backed securities for a limited period and may acquire assets related to such issuance, (2) acquire short-term securities for the purpose of maintaining the rating required by section 204, and (3) invest in Treasury obligations of maturities appropriate for satisfying claims of holders of enterprise debt obligations and mortgage-backed securities outstanding on the dissolution date; generally limits issuance of debt obligations that mature after the fifth anniversary of the enactment date.

Section 202. Disposing of assets

Sets fixed schedule, starting on the enactment date, for disposing of assets at a rate of at least five percent per calendar quarter and completely by the end of five years after the enactment date; prescribes an offset fee for each calendar quarter that the enterprise fails to meet the asset disposition schedule; fee is 0.25 percent of excess assets in the first year after the enactment date, 0.30 percent in the second year, 0.40 percent in the third year, 0.50 percent in the fourth year, and 0.60 percent in the fifth year; requires the enterprise to pay the fee into the Offset Fund within 30 days of the calendar quarter for which a payment is due.

Section 203. Mortgage-backed securities

Sets fixed schedule, starting 180 days after the enactment date, for reducing the amount of new mortgage-backed securities an enterprise may issue; schedule is set at a rate of ten percent per calendar quarter; requires each enterprise to cease issuing mortgage-backed securities or other financial products or services other than debt offerings approved by the Secretary of the Treasury by the end of thirty-six months after the enactment date. Provides that mortgage-backed securities or other financial products or services, other than debt offerings approved by the Secretary of the Treasury issued after the end of thirty-six months after the enactment date, shall be deemed to be null and void; prescribes an offset fee for each month that the enterprise fails to meet the asset disposition schedule; fee is 0.10 percent of excess assets in the first year, 0.15 percent in the second year, and 0.25 percent in the third year; requires the enterprise to pay the fee into the Offset Fund within 30 days of the calendar quarter for which a payment is due.

Section 204. Enterprise financial strength

Requires the regulator to hire two rating agencies at least annually to assess the financial condition of each enterprise without regard to any ties of the enterprise to the government; requires each enterprise to endeavor to achieve an "AA" rating, or the equivalent, without regard to ties to the government, from both rating agencies; prohibits an enterprise from transferring any property to the holding company created pursuant to section 206 if such transfer would cause the rating category to fall below that level; provides that, if an enterprise fails to maintain the "AA" rating, the holding company created pursuant to section 206 shall promptly transfer to the enterprise sufficient capital to restore that rating.

Section 205. Automated underwriting systems and mortgage and borrower databases

Requires each enterprise, within six months of the enactment date, to establish an independent corporation and transfer to the corporation without cost complete copies of all of the enterprise's automated underwriting systems software and the enterprise's complete information databases relating to characteristics of mortgages, or other extensions of credit, residential property, and borrowers; permits each enterprise to retain a copy of the systems and databases that it transfers to the corporation; requires each enterprise to distribute shares of the corporation pro rata to its shareholders as a dividend; requires the enterprise to enter into a contract to replenish and update the databases from time to time, but prohibits other contracts or other relationship between the enterprise (or its holding company) and the corporations that the two enterprises are required to establish under this section; requires each of the independent corporations to provide access for market participants and other interested parties to the automated underwriting systems and information databases on nondiscriminatory terms and conditions and at nondiscriminatory prices; permits each enterprise to retain a copy of the systems and databases that it transfers to the corporation.

Section 206. Reorganization through the formation of a holding company

Authorizes the board of directors of each enterprise to take action to create a holding company such that, upon shareholder approval, the holding company shall acquire all outstanding common shares of the enterprise and the shareholders of the enterprise will become shareholders of the holding company; provides that the holding company shall be established under the law of a state or the District of Columbia; provides for a majority of the holders of the enterprise's common stock to approve the plan of reorganization; requires that, before a holding company may engage in any business activities, the regulator shall certify that the enterprise has achieved the rating established by section 204 and that it has complied with the requirements of section 205, to create a separate corporation to make systems and databases available to interested parties on nonpreferential terms.

If the regulator makes the needed certification and shareholders approve the plan, authorizes the enterprise to transfer property to the holding company, subject to the requirements of section 204; provides that employees of the enterprise shall become employees of the holding company and that the holding company shall provide all necessary and appropriate operational support to the enterprise and shall pay the salaries and compensation of all employees, including those assigned to assist the enterprise; permits the enterprise to pay dividends so long as the Director determines, based on certification by the enterprise, that the enterprise would be in compliance with the requirements of section 204 after such payment.

Requires the enterprise to maintain books and records that clearly reflect the assets and liabilities of the enterprise as separate from the holding company or any subsidiary of the holding company; requires the enterprise to maintain an office that is physically separate from any office of the holding company or a subsidiary; requires that one officer of the enterprise shall be an officer solely of the enterprise; prohibits the enterprise from extending credit to or providing any credit enhancement for the holding company or any subsidiary of the holding company; provides that amounts the holding company collects on behalf of the enterprise shall be immediately deposited into an account under sole control of the enterprise; provides that, notwithstanding any federal or state law, rule, or regulation, or legal or equitable principle to the contrary, under no circumstances shall assets of the enterprise be available or used to pay claims or debts of or incurred by the holding company; requires all business activities of the holding company to be conducted through subsidiaries of the holding company.

Terminates the authority of the President of the United States to appoint five of the directors of an enterprise, effective at the end of the annual term of the directors during which the enactment date occurs; provides that no director of an enterprise who is appointed by the President may serve at the same time as a director of the holding company; prohibits the holding company from selling, pledging, or transferring shares of the enterprise or from agreeing to the liquidation of the enterprise without approval of the regulator.

Authorizes the holding company to prescribe the composition of its board of directors in its charter or bylaws, as permitted under applicable state law; prohibits use of the names "Federal National Mortgage Association" and "Federal Home Loan Mortgage Corporation"; permits the holding companies to use the name "Fannie Mae" or "Freddie Mac" after the dissolution date and requires certain disclosures for five years after the dissolution date; authorizes the regulator or the Secretary of the Treasury to enforce this act and authorizes the United States District Court to apply specified remedies and sanctions.

Section 207. Sunset

Provides for dissolution of the enterprise on the fifth anniversary of the enactment date, or such earlier date as the regulator may approve; requires the enterprise to establish trusts for the defeasance of enterprise debt obligations and mortgage-backed securities; to the extent that an enterprise cannot provide the amount of money or qualifying obligations required and, if a holding company has been established pursuant to this Act, requires the holding company to provide them; provides that any obligations of the enterprise that cannot be fully satisfied shall become liabilities of the holding company; provides that, after full satisfaction of all outstanding obligations and compliance with these dissolution requirements, any remaining assets of the trusts shall be transferred to the holding company or a subsidiary.

If there is no holding company, requires the enterprise to liquidate any remaining assets, satisfy outstanding obligations, and transfer the net proceeds to enterprise shareholders; provides that, on the dissolution date of each enterprise, its charter act shall be null and void except with respect to rights and obligations of any holders of outstanding enterprise debt obligations and mortgage-backed securities.

Section 208. Offset fund

Requires the regulator to establish a fund and to allocate to that fund all fees and other payments by the enterprises pursuant to this Act; after creation of a nonprofit affordable housing corporation pursuant to section 305, the Director shall allocate all funds to that corporation.

TITLE III—PRIVATIZATION OF THE FEDERAL HOME LOAN BANKS

Section 301. Restrictions on new activities and acquisition of assets

Prohibits the Banks or the System from engaging in new business activities, except for advances issued pursuant to section 302 and debt offerings approved by the Secretary of the Treasury, or from issuing any new obligations or guarantees or acquiring new assets, except for (1) short-term securities acquired for the purpose of maintaining the rating required by section 303, and (2) investment in Treasury obligations of maturities appropriate for use in satisfying the claims of holders of System or Bank debt obligations outstanding on the dissolution date; generally limits issuance of debt obligations to those that mature after the fifth anniversary of the enactment date.

Section 302. New advances; disposing of assets other than advances

Authorizes Banks to issue advances only if they are secured by collateral rated in one of the top two rating categories and mature before the fifth anniversary of the enactment date. Sets fixed schedule, starting 180 days after the enactment date, for reducing the amount of new advances a Bank may issue; schedule is set at a rate of ten percent per calendar quarter; requires the Banks and the System to cease issuing advances or other financial products or services other than debt offerings approved by the Secretary of the Treasury by the end of thirty-six months after the enactment date; provides that advances or other financial products or services, other than debt offerings approved by the Secretary of the Treasury, issued after the end of thirty-six months after the enactment date shall be deemed to be null and void.

Sets a fixed schedule, starting on the enactment date, for disposing of assets other than advances at a rate of at least five percent per calendar quarter and completely by the end of five years after the enactment date; prescribes an offset fee for each calendar quarter that the Bank fails to meet the asset disposition schedule; fee is 0.25 percent of excess assets in the first year, 0.30 percent in the second year, 0.40 percent in the third year, 0.50 percent in the fourth year, and 0.60 percent in the fifth year; requires the Bank to pay the fee into the Offset Fund within thirty days of the calendar quarter for which a payment is due.

Section 303. Bank financial strength

Requires the regulator to hire two rating agencies at least annually to assess the financial condition of each Bank and the System without regard to any ties of the Bank to other parts of the System or of the Banks and the System to the government, and to assess the financial condition of the System; requires each Bank to endeavor to achieve at least an "AA" rating, or the equivalent, without regard to ties to the government, from both rating agencies.

Effective on the date that the Congress begins deliberation on this Act, prohibits a Bank from permitting redemption of any stock until the Bank achieves an "AA" rating; allows the Bank to permit a redemption of stock only if, in the opinion of the regulator, after such redemption the Bank would remain in compliance with this section; prohibits a Bank from transferring any property to the holding company created pursuant to section 304 if such transfer would cause the rating category to fall below that level; provides that, if a Bank fails to maintain the "AA" rating, the holding company created pursuant to section 304 shall promptly transfer to the Bank sufficient capital to restore that rating.

Section 304. Reorganization through the formation of a holding company

Authorizes the board of directors of each Bank to take action to create a holding company such that, upon shareholder approval, the holding company shall acquire all outstanding common shares of the Bank and the shareholders of the Bank will become shareholders of the holding company; provides that the holding company shall be established under the law of a state or the District of Columbia; provides for a majority of the holders of the Bank's common stock to approve the plan of reorganization; requires that, before a holding company may engage in any business activities, the regulator shall certify that the Bank has achieved the rating established by section 303.

If the regulator makes the needed certification and shareholders approve the plan, authorizes the Bank to transfer property to the holding company, subject to the requirements of section 303; provides that employees of the Bank shall become employees of the holding company and that the holding company shall provide all necessary and appropriate operational support to the Bank and shall pay the salaries and compensation of all employees, including those assigned to assist the Bank; permits the Bank to pay dividends so long as the Director determines, based on certification by the Bank, that the Bank would be in compliance with the requirements of section 303 after such payment; requires the holding company to transfer to a Bank that fails to achieve the required rating sufficient added capital as needed to ensure that the Bank again complies with the requirements of this section.

Requires the Bank to maintain books and records that clearly reflect the assets and liabilities of the Bank as separate from the holding company or any subsidiary of the holding company; requires the Bank to maintain an office that is physically separate from any office of the holding company or a subsidiary; requires that one officer of the Bank shall be an officer solely of the Bank; prohibits the Bank from extending credit to or providing any credit enhancement for the holding company or any subsidiary of the holding company; provides that amounts the holding company collects on behalf of the Bank shall be immediately deposited into an account under sole control of the Bank; provides that, notwithstanding any federal or state law, rule, or regulation, or legal or equitable principle to the contrary, under no circumstances shall assets of the Bank be available or used to pay claims or debts of or incurred by the holding company; requires all business activities of the holding company to be conducted through subsidiaries of the holding company.

Terminates the authority of the regulator to appoint directors of any Bank, effective at the end of the annual term of the directors during which the enactment date occurs; provides that no director of a Bank who is appointed by the regulator pursuant to the Federal Home Loan Bank Act may serve at the same time as a director of the holding company; prohibits the holding company from selling, pledging, or transferring shares of the Bank or from agreeing to the liquidation of the Bank, without approval of the regulator.

Authorizes the holding company to prescribe the composition of its board of directors in its charter or bylaws, as permitted under applicable state law; prohibits use of the names "Federal Home Loan Bank" or "bank" or any form of words implying a connection to the United States Government; requires certain disclosures for five years after the dissolution date; authorizes the regulator or the Secretary of the Treasury to enforce this act and authorizes the United States District Court to apply specified remedies and sanctions.

Section 305. Sunset
Provides for dissolution of each Bank on the fifth anniversary of the enactment date, or such earlier date as the regulator may approve; requires the Bank to establish one or more trusts for the defeasance of Bank debt obligations; to the extent that a Bank cannot provide the amount of money or qualifying obligations required and, if a holding company has been established pursuant to this Act, requires the holding company to provide them; provides that any obligations of the Bank that cannot be fully satisfied shall become liabilities of the holding company; provides that, after full satisfaction of all outstanding obligations and compliance with these dissolution requirements, any remaining assets of the trust or trusts shall be transferred to the holding company or a subsidiary.

If there is no holding company, requires the Bank to liquidate any remaining assets, satisfy any remaining obligations, and transfer the net proceeds to the shareholders; requires dissolution of the System when the last Bank has been dissolved; requires the System to liquidate any remaining assets, satisfy any remaining obligations, and transfer the net proceeds on an equitable basis, as the regulator determines, to the holding companies operating pursuant to section 304.

Provides that, on the dissolution date, the Federal Home Loan Bank Act shall be null and void except with respect to rights and obligations of any holders of outstanding Bank debt obligations; before the dissolution date, requires the regulator to dissolve the Affordable Housing Reserve Fund, cause the establishment of an independent nonprofit corporation chartered under the laws of the District of Columbia for the purpose of providing financial assistance for affordable housing, and to transfer to the new corporation all funds held by or for the Affordable Housing Reserve Fund; requires the regulator, to the extent practicable, to request each holding company to select one representative to be a director of the nonprofit corporation.

Section-by-Section Summary:
The Mortgage Holding Subsidiary Act

Bert Ely

Section 2. Short title and table of contents

TITLE IV—AUTHORIZATION FOR INSURED DEPOSITORY INSTITUTIONS AND HOLDING COMPANIES TO OWN OR CONTROL MORTGAGE HOLDING SUBSIDIARIES

A federally insured commercial bank or thrift institution, a bank holding company, or a financial holding company would be permitted to form one or more mortgage holding subsidiaries (MHSs) that it could own in whole or in part. The exclusive activity of an MHS would be to own and finance residential mortgages with funds raised in the capital markets. This title of the Federal Housing Enterprises Privatization Act is modeled on and parallels the construction of 12 U.S.C. 24a, which was enacted by the Gramm-Leach-Bliley Act of 1999, authorizing national banks to establish financial subsidiaries.

Section 401. Definitions

Appropriate federal banking agency. The appropriate federal banking agency, as that term is defined in 12 U.S.C. 1813(q), is the agency charged with the primary responsibility for supervising and regulating an insured depository institution or a holding company. The Comptroller of the Currency is the primary federal regulator for national banks, District banks, and any Federal branch or agency of a foreign bank; the Office of Thrift Supervision is the primary federal regulator for thrift institutions; and the Federal Deposit Insurance Corporation is the primary federal regulator for state nonmember commercial banks and foreign banks with insured branches not regulated by the Comptroller. The Board of Governors of the Federal Reserve System, among its other supervisory responsibilities, is the primary federal regulator for state member banks, bank holding companies, financial holding companies, and foreign banks operating in the United States that do not have an FDIC-insured branch.

Federal banking agency. A federal banking agency is defined in 12 U.S.C. 1813(z). These agencies are the Office of the Comptroller of the Currency, the Director of the Office of Thrift Supervision, the Board of Governors of the Federal Reserve System, and the Federal Deposit Insurance Corporation.

Holding company. A holding company is a bank holding company, as that term is defined in 12 U.S.C. 1841(a) or a financial holding company, as that term is defined in 12 U.S.C. 1841(p). A financial holding company is merely a bank holding company that has met the requirements necessary to engage in expanded financial activities, as specified in 12 U.S.C. 1841(l)(1). The term "holding company" does not include savings and loan holding companies, as they are defined in 12 U.S.C. 1467a(1)(D).

Insured credit union. The term "insured credit union" is defined in 12 U.S.C. 1752(7). It encompasses federally chartered credit unions and state-chartered credit unions insured by the National Credit Union Share Insurance Fund (NCUSIF). This term does not include state-chartered credit unions not insured by the NCUSIF.

Insured depository institution. The term "insured depository institution" is defined in 12 U.S.C. 1813(c)(2). It encompasses national banks, state-chartered commercial banks, and thrift institutions, which include federally chartered savings associations and savings banks and comparable state-chartered thrift institutions.

Mortgage. A "mortgage" is defined as any recorded security interest on real estate (land and improvements thereto), whether a first mortgage or a junior mortgage. Hence, this definition includes a second mortgage or deed of trust securing a home equity loan, a home equity line of credit, or any other form of secured indebtedness on real estate.

Mortgage holding subsidiary. An MHS shall be a state-chartered general business corporation authorized to operate for profit. An MHS can be chartered by a state, the District of Columbia, Puerto Rico, or a U.S. territory. It must be permitted by state law to engage in the mortgage business, specifically owning, servicing, or securitizing residential mortgages. Since MHSs are envisioned as passive financing vehicles, they are not authorized to originate mortgages—that activity will be conducted by the MHS's parent or affiliate bank or thrift, holding company, or third parties, such as mortgage brokers. There would be no limit on the number of MHSs which can exist, who could own an MHS, how many equity owners an MHS could have, classes of stock it could issue, or forms of debt it could issue.

Mortgage holding subsidiary parent. An MHS parent is a federally insured commercial bank or thrift institution, a bank holding company, or a financial holding company, as those terms are defined and used in this title.

Residential property. The definition of residential properties encompasses not only owner-occupied single-family residences, but also two- to four-family homes, apartments, residential property available for rent, second homes, manufactured housing, and institutional housing, such as college dormitories and nursing homes. Because some housing is located within mixed-use buildings, such as an apartment house with stores or offices on the first floor, this definition has been broadened to include properties where nonresidential uses account for up to one-fourth the value of the buildings and improvements financed by the mortgage.

Securitizing mortgages. "Securitizing mortgages" encompasses two forms of securitization in which an MHS may engage: (1) selling a mortgage to a third-party trust which in turn sells security interests in mortgages owned by the trust and (2) "in-situ securitization," whereby the MHS sells to investors security interests in a group or pool of mortgages in which the MHS has retained ownership of the mortgages and then guarantees the timely payment of principal and interest on the securitized mortgages. In order to strengthen the security interest of investors in in-situ securities, MHS may elect to form a subsidiary to own the mortgages financed by a specific in-situ securities offering.

State. The term "State" encompasses all fifty states of the United States, the District of Columbia, Puerto Rico, and all territories of the United States, including Guam, American Samoa, the Trust Territory of the Pacific Islands, the Virgin Islands, and the Northern Mariana Islands.

Well capitalized and adequately capitalized. The terms "well capitalized" and "adequately capitalized" are defined in 12 U.S.C. 1831o, Prompt Corrective Action, in subparagraphs (b)(1)(A) and (B).

Section 402. Mortgage holding subsidiary

Mortgage holding subsidiary authorized. This paragraph authorizes a commercial bank, thrift institution, or bank or financial holding company to own, control, or hold an equity interest in one or several MHSs, as defined in section 401 of this title. There would be no limit on the number of MHSs which a commercial bank, thrift institution, or bank or financial holding company could own, control, or hold an equity interest in.

Permitted activities. In addition to such powers an MHS may hold from the state which chartered it, an MHS is specifically permitted under federal law and regulations to:

> (1) share directors, officers, employees, and facilities, such as buildings, computers, and computer software, with any party, including a commercial bank, thrift institution, or bank or financial holding company, which holds an equity ownership interest in the MHS;

(2) purchase mortgages from any mortgage originator, including any equity owner of the MHS, or in the secondary mortgage market, provided that the mortgage is on real estate located within the jurisdiction of a United States court;

(3) issue unsecured debt and guarantees which have a liquidation and bankruptcy preference over other unsecured debt, guarantees, and obligations of the MHS, excluding claims of the appropriate federal banking agency arising under section 403(a)(3) of this title, with the intention of using preferential debt principally to finance mortgages the MHS owns and preferential guarantees to support the MHS's in-situ securitizations; and

(4) grant a security interest in mortgages the MHS finances through in-situ securitization by issuing security interests in a group or pool of mortgages where the MHS retains ownership of the mortgages and then guarantees the timely payment of principal and interest on the securitized mortgages.

Prohibited activities. An MHS is expressly prohibited from:

(1) engaging in any activity, as an equity owner, not directly related to owning, servicing, or securitizing mortgages on residential properties;

(2) accepting deposits in any form whatsoever, whether those deposits are payable within the United States or elsewhere in the world;

(3) selling any form of debt to an individual in an amount less than $100,000; or

(4) doing anything that conveys in any way to the general public or to owners of the debt or other obligations of the MHS, including guarantees issued by the MHS, that the debt, guarantees, or other obligations are guaranteed or backed in any manner by any federally insured depository institution

(including credit unions), bank or financial holding company, or a federal deposit insurance agency.

Mortgage holding subsidiary not subject to banklike regulation. Because an MHS cannot be chartered as a depository institution; because it cannot accept deposits in any form; and because its debt, guarantees, and other obligations are not insured or otherwise guaranteed by any agency of the federal government, an MHS cannot be regulated by any federal banking agency. However, the appropriate federal banking agency is authorized to enforce on MHS owned or controlled by a commercial bank, thrift institution, or bank or financial holding company the MHS prohibitions specified in subsection 402(c) of this title.

Applicability of Federal and State laws. MHSs, as state-chartered general business corporations, will be subject to all federal and state laws to which comparable corporations are subject, specifically as those laws relate to an MHS's mortgage-related activities. Hence, while the states cannot generally regulate the activities of the subsidiaries of a national bank or federally chartered thrift institution, that would not be true of the MHS subsidiaries of a national bank or federally chartered thrift.

Unlike government-sponsored enterprises, MHSs would not be exempt from any federal laws. For example, MHS debt would not be exempt from limitations on the amount that a bank or thrift can lend to or invest in the debt of a business. Likewise, MHS debt or guaranteed obligations would not be eligible for Federal Reserve open market purchases or as collateral for public deposits. Additionally, MHSs would be subject to all laws administered by the Securities and Exchange Commission, including the Securities Act of 1933, the Securities Exchange Act of 1934, the Trust Indenture Act of 1939, and the Sarbanes-Oxley Act of 2002.

Importantly, MHSs would be subject in all regards to the U.S. Bankruptcy Code (Title 11) to ensure that no MHS or set of MHSs could cause systemic disruption to the U.S. financial system. Specifically, should an MHS become insolvent or be unable to pay its debts or other obligations in a timely manner, it could become either a voluntary or involuntary debtor under the Code, in which case the Code's automatic stay

(11 U.S.C. 362) would immediately freeze payment of all unsecured debt and other obligations of the MHS, except payments due under swap agreements and certain other contracts. Hence, there could not be a "run" on an MHS. Further, the MHS's debtor-in-possession could obtain post-petition credit under the provisions of 11 U.S.C. 364 so as to maintain the ongoing operations of the MHS.

Section 403. Safeguards for the mortgage holding subsidiary parent
This section contains prohibitions on the parent bank, thrift, or holding company. In order to protect a commercial bank, thrift institution, or bank or financial holding company from the activities of an MHS which might threaten the safe-and-sound operation or the solvency of the bank, thrift, or holding company, the parent of the MHS is barred from:

(1) entering into any transaction with an MHS in which it has an equity ownership interest which would violate the provisions of sections 23A and 23B of the Federal Reserve Act;

(2) guaranteeing or otherwise protecting from loss any debt, guarantee, or other obligation of any MHS which the bank, thrift, or holding company owns or controls or in which it holds an equity interest; or

(3) making an equity investment in any MHS, after which investment the bank, thrift, or holding company would be less-than-well-capitalized, after applying the capital deduction rule specified in section 404 of this title.

The second subparagraph complements paragraph 402(c)(4) of this title, which bars an MHS from claiming that its debt, guarantees, or other obligations are in any way guaranteed or otherwise protected from loss by any federally insured depository institution (including credit unions), a bank or financial holding company, or a federal deposit insurance agency.
The third subparagraph enables the appropriate federal banking agency to force an MHS to return to a commercial bank, thrift institution, or bank or financial holding company any equity capital or subordinated

debt the bank, thrift, or holding company invested in the MHS which has the immediate effect of dropping the bank, thrift, or holding company from a well-capitalized status to a less-than-well-capitalized status, after taking into account the capital deduction rule in section 404 of this title. Until such time as the investment is returned to the bank, thrift, or holding company, the appropriate Federal banking agency shall have a claim on the unsecured assets of the MHS superior to all other unsecured claims on the MHS, including preferential debt and guarantees. So as to encourage a rapid return of the overinvestment, the appropriate Federal banking agency's claim will carry an interest rate equal to the current rate on the ninety-one-day Treasury bill plus six percent. If the appropriate Federal banking agency's claim is outstanding against an MHS should the MHS file for protection under the Bankruptcy Code, that claim shall immediately become due and payable, along with any unpaid interest.

Indemnification of a parent bank, thrift, or holding company arising from the activities of an MHS. An MHS will hold its parent commercial bank(s), thrift institution(s), or bank or financial holding companies harmless from any judgment against the parent or parents arising from the activities of the MHS. While such situations should be quite rare, this provision provides an additional protection for the capital of the parent bank, thrift, or holding company.

Authority of the appropriate federal banking agency. The appropriate federal banking agency shall have the right to examine the assets, liabilities, and operations of an MHS, but only to the extent necessary to (1) determine the degree to which the activities of the MHS might threaten the safe-and-sound operation or solvency of the commercial bank(s), thrift institution(s), or bank or financial holding company or companies that own or control the MHS, specifically to reduce the MHS parent or parents to a less-than-adequately capitalized status and (2) determine whether the MHS has engaged in or is engaged in any activities prohibited for MHSs in subsection 402(c) of this title.

If the appropriate Federal banking agency determines that the activities of an MHS threaten the safe-and-sound operation or the solvency of a parent commercial bank, thrift institution, or bank or financial holding company, it *cannot* take regulatory action against the MHS. Instead, after giving notice and holding a public hearing, the appropriate Federal banking agency may direct the MHS's parent or parents to take such actions as are feasible which would strengthen the balance sheet and operations of the MHS or, if that is not feasible, to divest all or a portion of its or their equity interest in the MHS.

Although an MHS is exempt from banklike regulation, an MHS is subject to the prohibitions spelled out in subsection 402(c) of this title. That enforcement task falls to the appropriate federal banking agency, utilizing its existing enforcement powers under Title 12 of the U.S. Code.

Section 404. Capital deduction

The capital deduction subsection closely parallels the capital deduction section of 12 U.S.C. 24a, financial subsidiaries of national banks.

Capital deduction required. The first paragraph of this section states that the subordinated debt and equity capital investment of a commercial bank, thrift institution, or bank or financial holding company in an MHS, including earnings retained in the MHS, will be deducted from the assets, tangible equity capital, and outstanding subordinated debt of the commercial bank, thrift institution, or bank or financial holding company. This deduction has the effect of ensuring that a bank, thrift, or holding company's equity and subordinated debt investment in an MHS are fully funded by equity capital and subordinated debt invested in the MHS parent and not by the parent's deposits or other debt. This requirement eliminates the potential for double-leveraging, that is, double-counting equity capital and subordinated debt, at the bank, thrift, or holding company level and again at the MHS level.

In order to properly exclude the effect of an MHS's balance sheet on regulatory capital ratios calculated for a commercial bank, thrift institution, or bank or financial holding company, the second paragraph provides that the assets and liabilities of an MHS will not be consolidated with the assets of a commercial bank, thrift institution, or bank or financial holding company (and its non-MHS subsidiaries) for regulatory capital purposes. This exclusion, coupled with the preceding subparagraph, has the effect of measuring the MHS parent's assets, liabilities, capital, and capital ratios for regulatory purposes, as if the MHS did not exist.

Financial statement disclosure of capital deduction. When a commercial bank, thrift institution, or bank or financial holding company publishes its financial statements on a consolidated basis, in accordance with generally accepted accounting principles, those statements will include the assets, liabilities, and equity capital of all MHSs owned or controlled by the bank, thrift, or holding company as if those MHSs were an integral part of the bank, thrift, or holding company. However, under this subsection, a commercial bank, thrift institution, or a bank or financial holding company that owns or controls MHSs also will publish financial statements that exclude the assets, liabilities, and capital of MHSs the bank, thrift, or holding company owns or controls. By extension, the income statement of the bank, thrift, or holding company will exclude the income, expenses, and profits of the MHS. Since MHSs will be subject to all federal securities laws, an MHS issuing debt which must be registered with the Securities and Exchange Commission will have to publish audited financial statements excluding the assets, liabilities, income, and expenses of its parent bank, thrift, or holding company.

Section 405. Regulations
Within 180 days after enactment of the GSE privatization legislation, each federal banking agency must publish for comment whatever regulations it needs to carry out the purposes of this title.

Section 406. Coordinated examination of mortgage holding subsidiaries
If an MHS is owned or controlled by insured depository institutions or holding companies supervised and regulated by more than one Federal banking agency, then those agencies shall coordinate their examination of the MHS so as to avoid duplicative examinations.

Section 407. Conforming amendments

Subsection (a) – Capital regulation. Because MHSs are not depository institutions and their liabilities are not federally insured, they must be exempt from all commercial bank, thrift institution, and bank and financial holding company regulation. Section 404 of this title effectively exempts MHSs from consolidated capital regulation of commercial banks, thrift institutions, and bank and financial holding companies. The first paragraph of this subsection excludes the assets, liabilities, and capital of MHSs from the capital requirements and prompt corrective action provisions of the Federal Deposit Insurance Act applicable to all federally insured depository institutions; that is, federally insured commercial banks and thrift institutions.

The second paragraph excludes the assets, liabilities, and capital of MHSs from the consolidated capital regulation administered by the Federal Reserve for bank and financial holding companies and state member banks. That is, when determining whether a bank or thrift meets its capital requirements and whether a holding company meets its consolidated capital requirements, the bank, thrift, or holding company shall be treated as if the MHS did not exist.

Subsection (b) – Savings and loan holding company amendments. Two provisions in the savings and loan holding company statute (12 U.S.C. 1467a) must be amended to accommodate MHSs. First, subsection (c) of that section prohibits certain activities for a savings and loan holding company and its subsidiaries, direct and indirect, which are not thrift institutions (savings associations). So that MHSs will not run afoul of the subsection (c) prohibitions, MHSs are exempted from these prohibitions.

Second, thrift institutions are subject to a complex "qualified thrift lender," or QTL, test. If a thrift institution shifts many of the mortgages it owns into MHSs or sells most of its mortgage originations to its MHS, it might fail the QTL test. Therefore, to sidestep this problem, the legislation amends the definition of "qualified thrift investments" to provide that MHSs will be treated, for purposes of the QTL test, as if they were owned by the thrift institution. That is, just for the QTL test, the assets of the thrift's MHS are consolidated with the thrift's assets. If a thrift owns less than 100 percent of the voting stock of an MHS, then only that portion of the MHS's assets are consolidated with the thrift's assets for the purpose of the QTL test. For example, if a thrift owns 60 percent of the voting stock of an MHS, then for QTL proposes only 60 percent of each category of the MHS's assets would be consolidated with the comparable assets of the thrift institution.

Subsection (c) – Real estate appraisals. Because MHSs are not federally insured depository institutions, there is no reason that the Financial Institutions Reform, Recovery, and Enforcement Act real estate appraisal requirements should apply to MHSs. This subsection exempts MHSs from that appraisal requirement. Additionally, this subsection exempts federally insured banks and thrifts from the appraisal requirement when the bank or thrift intends and does in fact execute that sale to the MHS in a timely manner. That is, the bank or thrift cannot hold a mortgage intended for sale to an MHS for several years before executing that sale. However, this exemption would not apply in a situation where an MHS sells a mortgage to a bank or thrift, such as if an MHS resells a mortgage to the bank or thrift which originated the mortgage.

Subsection (d) – Community Reinvestment Act. Since MHSs will not be insured depository institutions, and since the Community Reinvestment Act (CRA) is intended to apply only to insured depository institutions, there is no rationale for applying the CRA to an MHS, just as the CRA has not been applied to nondepository affiliates of banks and thrifts or to nondepository financial firms.

Subsection (e) – Tying arrangements. Operationally, an MHS will be closely related to its parent bank(s), thrift(s), or holding companies. Therefore, an MHS should be no more restrained, in terms of how it integrates financial products and services with its parent banks(s), thrift(s), or holding companies than would be the case if the MHS were an integral part of its parent organization(s). Hence, this exemption from the antitying statutes, specifically Chapter 22 of Title 12, applies to bank and financial holding companies, banks and thrifts owned by bank and financial holding companies, and commercial banks not owned by holding companies, while 12 U.S.C. 1464(q) applies to savings associations such as savings and loans, savings banks, and the like not owned or controlled by a bank or financial holding company.

A BILL

To remove the government sponsorship of the Federal housing-related enterprises and permit their reorganization through the formation of holding companies

SECTION 1. SHORT TITLE AND TABLE OF CONTENTS.

(a) SHORT TITLE—This Act may be cited as the Federal Housing Enterprises Privatization Act.

(b) TABLE OF CONTENTS—The table of contents for this Act is as follows:

TITLE I—IMPROVEMENT OF SUPERVISION; DEFINITIONS

SECTION 101. SUPERVISION.

The Director [the supervisor and regulator of the enterprises and the Federal Home Loan Banks] shall have all necessary authority, including general regulatory authority, to discharge the responsibilities assigned to such Director by this Act, and to use all supervisory and enforcement authority available to the Director under existing law to assure that the purposes of this Act are carried out.

SECTION 102. DEFINITIONS.

(1) The term "automated underwriting system" includes, without limitation, any computerized or data processing system of underwriting that evaluates information about a potential borrower based on key attributes of the borrower, the property, or any other aspect of the credit transaction, and that predicts, alone or in conjunction with an evaluation of additional information, the likelihood of default, prepayment, or any other event that is relevant to the decision whether to purchase, service, sell, lend on

the security of, or otherwise deal in a mortgage, including any ancillary systems for automated valuation and other automated services related to mortgage origination.

(2) The term "Bank" means a Federal Home Loan Bank, including a Bank that is created as a result of merger or consolidation pursuant to this Act.

(3) The term "calendar quarter" means any three-month period, commencing on the first day of the first month and ending on the last day of the third month. The first month of any calendar quarter shall include any days of the preceding month that have not been included in a prior calendar quarter.

(4) The term "consolidated obligation" means a debt obligation of the Federal Home Bank System that is a joint and several obligation of all of the Federal Home Loan Banks.

(5) The term "Director" means the Director [supervisor and regulator] of the enterprises and Federal Home Loan Banks under Title I.

(6) The term "dissolution date" means the date five years after the date of enactment of this Act, or such earlier date as the Director permits, when an enterprise or Bank is dissolved in accordance with this Act.

(7) The term "enactment date" means the date of enactment of this Act.

(8) The term "enterprise" means the Federal National Mortgage Association ("Fannie Mae") and the Federal Home Loan Mortgage Corporation ("Freddie Mac"). The term "enterprise" shall not include any holding company created under this Act or any subsidiary of such holding company (other than the enterprise).

(9) The term "enterprise charter act" means either the Federal National Mortgage Association Charter Act or the Federal Home Loan Mortgage Corporation Charter Act, as the case may be.

(10) The term "holding company" means the new business corporation established pursuant to this Act by an enterprise or Bank under the laws of any State of the United States or the District of Columbia for the purposes of the reorganization and restructuring described in section 206 or section 304 of this Act.

(11) The term "information database" includes, without limitation, information relating to characteristics of borrowers, property, or mortgages or other extensions of credit that is taken from the mortgage application or from other mortgage documents, whether electronic or otherwise, or from other sources, including external sources such as credit bureaus, that is related to the likelihood of default, prepayment or any other event that is relevant to the decision whether to purchase, service, sell, lend on the security of, or otherwise deal in a mortgage or other extension of credit, including information related to automated valuation and other services ancillary to mortgage origination.

(12) The term "remaining obligations" means the debt obligations of an enterprise or Bank, including consolidated obligations issued or outstanding with respect to that Bank, that are outstanding as of the dissolution date.

(13) The term "remaining property" means the following assets and liabilities of an enterprise or Bank that are outstanding as of the reorganization effective date:

> (A) Debt obligations issued by the (i) enterprise or (ii) Bank or (iii) the System with respect to a Bank.

> (B) Contracts relating to interest rate, currency, or commodity positions or protections.

(C) Investment securities owned by the enterprise or Bank.

(D) Any instruments, assets, or agreements relating to the business of the enterprise or Bank.

(E) Except as specifically prohibited by this Act, any other assets or liabilities of the enterprise which the enterprise's or Bank's board of directors determines to be necessary or appropriate to the enterprise's operations.

(14) The term "reorganization" means the restructuring event or events (including any merger event) giving effect to the holding company structure described in section 206 or 304 of this section.

(15) The term "reorganization effective date" means the effective date of the reorganization under this Act as determined by the Board of Directors of the enterprise or Bank, which shall not be earlier than the date that shareholder approval is obtained pursuant to section 206 or section 304 and shall not be later than the dissolution date.

(16) The term "subsidiary" means one or more direct or indirect subsidiaries.

(17) The term "System" means the Federal Home Loan Bank System.

TITLE II—TERMINATION OF CERTAIN ACTIVITIES OF FANNIE MAE AND FREDDIE MAC

SECTION 201. RESTRICTIONS ON NEW ACTIVITIES AND ACQUISITION OF ASSETS.

(a) LOAN LIMITS –

(1) The Federal National Mortgage Association Charter Act is amended by adding at the end of the seventh sentence of

subsection 302(b)(2) the words, "and ending on [the enactment date]."

(2) Loan limits. The Federal Home Mortgage Association Charter Act is amended by adding at the end of the sixth sentence of subsection 305(a)(2) the words, "and ending on [the enactment date]."

(b) ACTIVITIES – Other than the issuance of (1) mortgage-backed securities for 180 days, and thereafter as limited by section 203, and (2) debt offerings approved by the Secretary of the Treasury pursuant to the enterprise charter acts, each enterprise shall not engage in any new business activities or acquire any additional assets, except (1) as such assets are related to the issuance of mortgage-backed securities under Section 203, (2) short-term securities acquired for the purpose of maintaining the rating required by section 204, and (3) investment in Treasury obligations of maturities appropriate for use in satisfying, pursuant to section 207 of this Act, the claims of holders of enterprise debt obligations and mortgage-backed securities outstanding on the dissolution date.

(c) DEBT OBLIGATIONS – After the enactment date, an enterprise shall not issue debt obligations which mature later than the fifth anniversary of the enactment date, except as the Secretary of the Treasury may approve.

SECTION 202. DISPOSING OF ASSETS.

(a) DISPOSITION SCHEDULE – Commencing on the enactment date, each enterprise shall dispose of its mortgages, mortgage-backed securities, and other investment assets according to a fixed schedule. Such disposition shall be made at a rate not less than five percent-per-calendar quarter of the principal amount of such assets held by the enterprise on the enactment date and as stated on the most recent quarterly balance sheet of the enterprise. Normal runoff of assets during any calendar quarter shall count toward the asset disposition obligation of the enterprise hereunder. Each enterprise shall completely dispose of such assets by the end of five years after the enactment date.

(b) OFFSET FEE – For each calendar quarter that the enterprise fails to meet the asset disposition schedule established by subsection (a), the enterprise shall be subject to an offset fee, which shall be applied to the average excess amount of assets held each year by the enterprise over the amount permitted by subsection (a). During the first year after the enactment date, the offset fee shall equal 0.25 percent per year of such excess assets, 0.30 percent during the second year after the enactment date, 0.40 percent during the third year after the enactment date, 0.50 percent for the fourth year, and 0.60 percent during the fifth year. The enterprise shall pay the offset fee into the Offset Fund within 30 days after the end of each calendar quarter after the enactment date for which any such fee is due.

SECTION 203. MORTGAGE-BACKED SECURITIES.

(a) SCHEDULE – Commencing 180 days after the enactment date, each enterprise shall reduce the amount of mortgage-backed securities that it issues according to a fixed schedule. Such reduction shall be made at a rate of ten percent-per-calendar quarter of the amount of such mortgage-backed securities issued by the enterprise and outstanding at the date which is 180 days after the date of enactment. Each enterprise shall completely cease issuing mortgage-backed securities, or offering any other financial products or services, at the end of thirty-six months after the enactment date, and any such issuances or offerings, other than debt offerings approved by the Secretary of the Treasury, shall be deemed to be null and void.

(b) OFFSET FEE – For each month that the enterprise fails to meet the thirty-month fixed schedule of reducing its issuance of mortgage-backed securities as provided in subsection (a), the enterprise shall be subject to an offset fee, which shall be applied to the average annual excess principal amount of mortgage-backed securities issued by the enterprise over the amount permitted by subsection (a). The offset fee shall be applied in an amount of 0.10 percent per year of such excess issuances during the first year after the enactment date, 0.15 percent during the second year after the enactment date, and 0.25 percent during the third year after the enactment date. The enterprise shall pay the offset fee into the Offset Fund within 30 days after the end of each calendar quarter after the enactment date for which any such fee is due.

SECTION 204. ENTERPRISE FINANCIAL STRENGTH.

(a) RATINGS – From time to time, but at least annually, the Director shall employ the services of two entities effectively recognized by the Division of Market Regulation of the Securities and Exchange Commission as nationally recognized statistical rating organizations for the purposes of the capital rules for broker dealers, each to conduct an assessment of the financial condition of each enterprise for the purpose of determining the credit risk of obligations issued by each enterprise, including senior obligations and subordinated obligations, without regard to any connection the enterprise may be deemed to have to the government or any form of financial backing of the enterprise other than that provided by the financial strength of the enterprise by itself.

(b) RATING CATEGORY – Within six months of the enactment date, each enterprise shall endeavor to achieve and maintain a senior debt rating that in the opinion of both rating organizations employed pursuant to subsection (a) is equivalent to the top category or to the middle range of the second category of ratings, i.e., at least an "AA" rating, or the equivalent thereof, generally assigned by the rating organizations to corporate debt. Such rating shall be made without regard to any connection that the enterprise may be deemed to have to the government or any form of financial backing of the enterprise other than that provided by the financial strength of the enterprise by itself.

(c) TRANSFERS – An enterprise shall not transfer any property, including real, personal, intellectual, and any other form of property, or any form of asset, including financial assets, to the holding company created pursuant to section 206 of this Act if such transfer would cause the rating category of the enterprise to fall below the rating prescribed by this section. If, at any time after the reorganization effective date, the enterprise fails to achieve such rating, the holding company within 90 days shall transfer to the enterprise additional capital in such amounts as are necessary to ensure that the enterprise again complies with the requirements of this section.

SECTION 205. AUTOMATED UNDERWRITING SYSTEMS AND MORTGAGE AND BORROWER DATABASES.

(a) INDEPENDENT COMPANY – Within six months of the enactment date, each enterprise shall establish a corporation and shall transfer to such corporation, without cost, complete copies of (1) all of the enterprise's automated underwriting systems software and (2) the enterprise's complete information databases relating to characteristics of mortgages, or other extensions of credit, residential property, and borrowers, including information related to automated valuation and other services ancillary to mortgage origination. Each enterprise may retain a copy of the systems and databases that it transfers to the corporation established under this subsection.

(b) OWNERSHIP AND CONTROL – Immediately after the transfer required by subsection (a) the enterprise shall (1) elect qualified persons to be the temporary board of directors of such corporation, none of whom shall have any connection, financial or otherwise, with either of the enterprises, and (2) distribute shares of such corporation pro rata to its shareholders, as a dividend. The enterprise shall enter into a contract with such corporation to replenish and update the information databases from time to time, but, until the dissolution date of the enterprise, neither the enterprise nor its holding company otherwise may enter into any contracts or other relationship with the corporation established under subsection (a) or with the similar corporation established by the other enterprise pursuant to this section.

(c) MARKET ACCESS – Each of the corporations established pursuant to subsection (a) shall provide access for market participants and other interested parties, through license agreements or otherwise, to the automated underwriting systems and information databases on nondiscriminatory terms and conditions and at nondiscriminatory prices.

SECTION 206. REORGANIZATION THROUGH THE FORMATION OF A HOLDING COMPANY.

(a) ACTIONS BY ENTERPRISE'S BOARD OF DIRECTORS – The board of directors of each enterprise may take or cause to be taken all such action as the board of directors deems necessary or appropriate to effect, upon the shareholder approval described in subsection (b) of this section, a reorganization of the ownership of the enterprise, such that a holding company established under the law of a State of the United States or the District of Columbia shall acquire full record and beneficial ownership of all the outstanding common shares of the enterprise, and the shareholders of record of the enterprise on the record date chosen by the board of directors shall become the shareholders of the holding company.

(b) SHAREHOLDER APPROVAL – The plan of reorganization adopted by the board of directors pursuant to subsection (a) of this section shall be submitted to common shareholders of the enterprise for their approval. The reorganization shall occur on the reorganization effective date, provided that such reorganization has been approved by the affirmative votes, cast in person or by proxy, of the holders of a majority of the issued and outstanding shares of the enterprise's common stock.

(c) CERTIFICATION AND TRANSITION – Before the holding company may engage in any business activities the Director shall certify that (1) the enterprise has achieved and maintains the rating category required by section 204 of this Act, and (2) that the enterprise has fully complied with the requirements of section 205 of this Act. In the event the director makes the necessary certification and shareholders of the enterprise approve the plan of reorganization under subsection (b) of this section, the following provisions shall apply beginning on the reorganization effective date:

(1) In general – Except as otherwise provided in this Act, and until the dissolution date, the enterprise shall continue to have all of the rights, privileges, and obligations set forth in, and shall be subject to all of the limitations and restrictions of, the enterprise charter act, and, to the extent authorized by this Act, the enterprise shall continue to carry out the purposes of such charter act. Neither the holding company nor any subsidiary of the holding company (other than the enterprise) shall be entitled to any of the rights and privileges, nor be subject to the obligations, limitations, and restrictions, applicable to the enterprise under the enterprise charter act, except as specifically provided in this Act.

(2) Transfer of certain property –

(A) In general – Except as provided in this section, and with approval of the Director, on the reorganization effective date or as soon as practicable thereafter, the enterprise may transfer or dividend to the holding company all real and personal property of the enterprise (both tangible and intangible) other than the remaining property; provided, however, that no such transfer or dividend, or all such transfers or dividends in the aggregate, shall in the opinion of the Director impair the ability of the enterprise to maintain an AA-equivalent rating as provided in section 204(b).

(B) Construction – Nothing in this paragraph shall be construed to prohibit the enterprise from transferring remaining property from time to time to the holding company or any subsidiary of the holding company, subject to the requirements of paragraph (4).

(3) Transfer of personnel – On the reorganization effective date, employees of the enterprise shall become employees of the holding company (or any subsidiary of the holding company), and the holding company (or any subsidiary of the holding company) shall provide all necessary and appropriate management and

operational support to the enterprise, as requested by the enterprise. The enterprise, however, may obtain such management and operational support from persons or entities not associated with the holding company. The holding company shall pay the salaries and other compensation for all employees of the holding company, including those from time to time assigned to assist the enterprise.

(4) Dividends – The enterprise may pay dividends in the form of cash or noncash distributions so long as, in the opinion of the Director, after giving effect to the payment of such dividends, the enterprise would be in compliance with the requirements of section 204(b) of this Act.

(5) Certification prior to dividend – Prior to the payment of any dividend under paragraph (4), the enterprise shall certify to the Director that the payment of the dividend will be made in compliance with paragraph (2) and shall provide copies of all calculations needed to make such certification.

(d) SEPARATE OPERATION OF CORPORATIONS –

(1) In general – The funds and assets of the enterprise shall at all times be maintained separately from the funds and assets of the holding company or any subsidiary of the holding company and may be used by the enterprise solely to carry out the enterprise's purposes and to fulfill the enterprise's obligations.

(2) Books and records – The enterprise shall maintain books and records that clearly reflect the assets and liabilities of the enterprise, separate from the assets and liabilities of the holding company or any subsidiary of the holding company.

(3) Corporate office – The enterprise shall maintain a corporate office that is physically separate from any office of the holding company or any subsidiary of the holding company.

(4) One officer requirement – At least one officer of the enterprise shall be an officer solely of the enterprise.

(5) Credit prohibition – The enterprise shall not extend credit to the holding company or any subsidiary of the holding company nor guarantee or provide any credit enhancement to any debt obligations of the holding company or any subsidiary of the holding company.

(6) Amounts collected – Any amounts collected on behalf of the enterprise by the holding company or any subsidiary of the holding company with respect to the assets of the enterprise, pursuant to a servicing contract or other arrangement between the enterprise and the holding company or any subsidiary of the holding company, shall be collected solely for the benefit of the enterprise and shall be immediately deposited by the holding company or such subsidiary to an account under the sole control of the enterprise.

(e) ENCUMBRANCE OF ASSETS – Notwithstanding any Federal or State law, rule, or regulation, or legal or equitable principle, doctrine, or theory to the contrary, under no circumstances shall the assets of the enterprise be available or used to pay claims or debts of or incurred by the holding company. Nothing in this section shall be construed to limit the right of the enterprise to pay dividends not otherwise prohibited under this section or to limit any liability of the holding company explicitly provided for in this section.

(f) HOLDING COMPANY ACTIVITIES – After the reorganization effective date and prior to the dissolution date, all business activities of the holding company shall be conducted through subsidiaries of the holding company (other than the enterprise).

(g) DIRECTORS –

(1) Fannie Mae – Subsection (b) of section 308 of the Federal National Mortgage Association Charter Act (12 U.S.C. 1723(b)) is amended—

(A) in the first sentence, by striking "five of whom shall be appointed annually by the President of the United States, and the remainder of whom" and inserting "who";

(B) in the second sentence, by striking "appointed by the President";

(C) in the third sentence—

(i) by striking "appointed or"; and

(ii) by striking ", except that any such appointed member may be removed from office by the President for good cause";

(D) in the fourth sentence, by striking "elective"; and

(E) by striking the fifth sentence.

(2) Freddie Mac – Paragraph (2) of section 303(a) of the Federal Home Loan Mortgage Corporation Act (12 U.S.C. 1452(a)(2)) is amended—

(A) in Subparagraph (A),

(i) in the first sentence, by striking "five of whom shall be appointed annually by the President of the United States, and the remainder of whom" and inserting "who"; and

(ii) in the second sentence, by striking "appointed by the President of the United States";

(B) in Subparagraph (B),

(i) by striking "such or"; and

(ii) by striking, "except that any appointed member may be removed from office by the President for good cause"; and

(C) in Subparagraph (C),

(i) by striking the first sentence; and

(ii) by striking "elective."

(3) Application – The amendments made by paragraphs (1) and (2) shall not apply to any appointed position of the board of directors of an enterprise until the expiration of the annual term for such position following the enactment date.

(4) Appointed directors – No director of the enterprise who is appointed by the President pursuant to the enterprise charter act may at the same time serve as a director of the holding company.

(h) RESTRICTIONS ON TRANSFER OF ENTERPRISE SHARES AND BANKRUPTCY OF THE ENTERPRISE – After the reorganization effective date, the holding company shall not sell, pledge, or otherwise transfer the outstanding shares of the enterprise, or agree to or cause the liquidation of the enterprise or cause the enterprise to file a petition for bankruptcy or insolvency, without prior approval of the Director.

(i) OPERATING THE HOLDING COMPANY –

(1) Board of directors of the holding company – The number of members and composition of the board of directors of the holding company shall be determined as set forth in the holding company's charter or like instrument (as amended from time to time) or bylaws (as amended from time to time) and as permitted under the laws of the jurisdiction of the holding company's incorporation.

(2) Holding company name – The name of the holding company of each enterprise and any subsidiary of the holding company (other than the enterprise) may not use any form of the name "Federal National Mortgage Association," or "Fannie Mae," or "Federal Home Loan Mortgage Corporation" or "Freddie Mac"; provided, however, that after the dissolution of the enterprises a holding company may, to the extent permitted by applicable State or District of Columbia law, use the name "Fannie Mae" or "Freddie Mac", as the case may be, or variations thereof, or such other names as the board of directors of the enterprise or the holding company deem appropriate.

(3) Disclosure required – Until five years after the dissolution date, the holding company, and any subsidiary of the holding company (other than the enterprise), shall prominently display –

(A) in any document offering the holding company's securities, a statement that (1) the obligations of the holding company and any subsidiary of the holding company are not guaranteed by the full faith and credit of the United States, and (2) the holding company is not a government-sponsored enterprise of the United States; and

(B) in any advertisement or promotional materials which use the "Fannie Mae" or "Freddie Mac" name or mark, a statement that neither the holding company nor any subsidiary of the holding company is a government-sponsored enterprise of the United States.

(j) STRICT CONSTRUCTION; RIGHT TO ENFORCE –

(1) Strict construction – Except as specifically set forth in this section, nothing in this section shall be construed to limit the authority of the enterprise as a federally chartered corporation, or of the holding company as a state or District of Columbia chartered corporation.

(2) Right to enforce – The Secretary of the Treasury or the Director, as appropriate, may request that the Attorney General bring an action in the United States District Court for the District of Columbia for the enforcement of any provision of this section, or may directly bring such an action. Such court shall have jurisdiction and power to order and require compliance with this section, to seek injunctive relief, and to impose civil money penalties on the enterprises, the holding companies, and their officers and directors for willful failure to comply with the provisions of this Act.

SECTION 207. SUNSET.

(a) DISSOLUTION OF THE ENTERPRISES –

(1) Termination – Each enterprise shall dissolve, and the enterprise's separate existence shall terminate on the fifth anniversary of the date of enactment of this Act, after discharge of all outstanding debt obligations and liquidation pursuant to this subsection. The enterprise may dissolve pursuant to this subsection prior to such date by notifying the Director of the enterprise's intention to dissolve, and upon the Director's determination that all necessary steps have been or will be taken to protect creditors, holders of mortgage-backed securities, or others prior to such dissolution. On or before the dissolution date, the enterprise shall take the following actions:

(A) Establishment of one or more trusts for enterprise debt obligations – Not later than the fifth anniversary of the enactment date, each enterprise shall, under the terms of one or more irrevocable trust agreements that are in form and substance satisfactory to the Secretary of the Treasury and the appointed trustee or trustees, irrevocably transfer all remaining debt obligations of the enterprise to a trust or trusts and irrevocably deposit or cause to be deposited into such trust or trusts, to be held as trust funds solely for the benefit of holders of the remaining obligations, money or direct noncallable obligations of the United States or any agency thereof for which payment the full faith and credit of the United States is pledged, maturing as to principal and interest in such amounts and at such times as are determined by the Secretary of the Treasury to be sufficient, without consideration of any significant reinvestment of such interest, to pay the principal of, and interest on, the remaining obligations in accordance with their terms. To the extent the enterprise cannot provide money or qualifying obligations in the amount required, and if the enterprise has created a holding company that operates pursuant to this Act, the holding company shall be required to transfer money or qualifying obligations to the trust or trusts in the amount necessary to prevent any deficiency. All money, obligations, or financial assets deposited into the trust or trusts pursuant to this subsection shall be applied by the trustee or trustees to the payment of the remaining obligations assumed by the trust.

(B) Establishment of mortgage trusts – Not later than the fifth anniversary of the enactment date, each enterprise shall irrevocably transfer or cause to be transferred to one or more trusts all mortgages held for the purpose of backing outstanding mortgage-backed securities, under the terms of one or more irrevocable trust agreements that are in form and substance satisfactory to the Secretary of the Treasury and the appointed trustee or trustees, and shall irrevocably deposit or cause to be deposited into such trust or trusts, to be held as trust funds solely for the benefit of holders of the remaining mortgage-backed securities, money, or direct noncallable obligations of the United States or any agency thereof for which payment the full faith and credit of the United States is pledged, maturing as to principal and interest in such amounts and at such times as are determined by the Secretary of the Treasury to be sufficient, without consideration of any significant reinvestment of such interest, to pay the principal of, and interest on, the remaining mortgage-backed securities in accordance with their terms, after taking account of the mortgages transferred to the trust or trusts pursuant to this section. To the extent the enterprise cannot provide money or qualifying obligations in the amount required, if the enterprise has created a holding company that operates pursuant to this Act, the holding company shall be required to transfer money or qualifying obligations to the trust in the amount necessary to prevent any deficiency. All money, obligations, or financial assets deposited into the trust or trusts pursuant to this subsection shall be applied by the trustee or trustees to the payment of the remaining obligations assumed by the trust.

(C) Obligations not transferred to the trusts – The enterprise shall make proper provision for all other obligations of the enterprise not transferred to the trusts, including the repurchase or redemption, or the making of proper provision for the repurchase or redemption, of any preferred stock of the enterprise outstanding. If an enterprise has created a holding company that operates pursuant to this Act, any obligations of the enterprise which cannot be fully satisfied shall become liabilities of the holding company as of the date of dissolution.

(D) Transfer of remaining assets – If an enterprise has created a holding company that operates pursuant to this Act, after compliance with paragraphs (A) through (C), any remaining assets of the trust shall be transferred to the holding company or any subsidiary of the holding company, as directed by the holding company. In the event an enterprise does not operate a holding company pursuant to this Act, the enterprise shall liquidate any remaining assets, satisfy all remaining obligations of the enterprise that have not otherwise been provided for, and transfer the net proceeds of such liquidation to its shareholders on a pro rata basis.

(b) REPEAL OF CHARTER ACTS – On the dissolution date of each enterprise, its charter act shall be null and void except with respect to rights and obligations of any holders of outstanding enterprise debt obligations and mortgage-backed securities.

SECTION 208. OFFSET FUND.

The Director shall establish a fund, to be known as the Offset Fund, and shall place all amounts paid by the enterprises from offset fees and other payments by the enterprises under this Act into the fund. Upon creation of a not-for-profit affordable housing corporation pursuant to section 305 of this Act, and promptly thereafter, the Director shall allocate all monies in the Offset Fund to such corporation.

TITLE III—PRIVATIZATION OF THE FEDERAL HOME LOAN BANKS

SECTION 301. RESTRICTIONS ON NEW ACTIVITIES AND ACQUISITION OF ASSETS.

(a) ACTIVITIES – On and after the enactment date, other than advances authorized pursuant to section 302, and debt offerings approved by the Secretary of the Treasury, neither the System nor individual Banks shall engage in any new business activities or issue any new obligations or guarantees or acquire any additional assets, except (1) short-term securities acquired for the purpose of maintaining the rating required by section 303, and (2) investment in Treasury obligations of maturities appropriate for use in satisfying, pursuant to section 305 of this Act, the claims of holders of System or Bank debt obligations outstanding on the dissolution date.

(b) DEBT OBLIGATIONS – On and after the enactment date, neither Banks nor the System shall issue debt obligations which mature later than the fifth anniversary of the enactment date, except as the Secretary of the Treasury may approve.

SECTION 302. NEW ADVANCES; DISPOSING OF ASSETS OTHER THAN ADVANCES.

(a) NEW ADVANCE BUSINESS – Effective on the enactment date, each Bank may issue advances, pursuant to section 10 of the Federal Home Loan Bank Act (12 U.S.C. 1430), only if such advances are secured by eligible collateral that is sufficient to achieve a senior debt rating that is equivalent to the top category or to the middle range of the second category of ratings, i.e., at least the "AA" rating, or the equivalent thereof, assigned by a nationally recognized statistical rating organization, and if such advances have a maturity date of not later than the fifth anniversary of the enactment date.

(b) SCHEDULE – Commencing 180 days after the enactment date, each Bank shall reduce the amount of its permitted advances according to a fixed schedule. Such reduction shall be made at a rate of ten percent-per-calendar quarter of the amount of such advances issued by the Bank at the date which is 180 days after the date of enactment. Each Bank and the System shall completely cease issuing advances, or offering any other financial products or services, by the end of thirty-six months after the enactment date, and any such issuances or offerings after such thirty-six-month period, other than debt offerings approved by the Secretary of the Treasury, shall be deemed to be null and void.

(c) DISPOSITION OF ASSETS OTHER THAN ADVANCES – Commencing on the enactment date, each Bank shall dispose of its assets, other than advances issued pursuant to section 10 of the Federal Home Loan Bank Act (12 U.S.C. 1430), according to a fixed schedule. Such disposition shall be made at a rate not less than five percent-per-calendar quarter, of the principal amount of such assets held by the Bank on the enactment date and as stated on the most recent quarterly balance sheet of the Bank. Normal runoff of assets during any calendar quarter shall count toward the asset disposition obligation of the Bank hereunder. Each Bank shall completely dispose of such assets by the end of five years after the enactment date.

(d) OFFSET FEE – For each calendar quarter that a Bank fails to meet the asset disposition schedule established by subsection (c), the Bank shall be subject to an offset fee, which shall be applied to the average excess amount of assets held each year by the Bank over the amount permitted by subsection (c). During the first year after the enactment date, the offset fee shall equal 0.25 percent per year of such excess assets, 0.30 percent during the second year, 0.40 percent during the third year after the enactment date, 0.50 percent for the fourth year, and 0.60 percent during the fifth year. The Bank shall pay the offset fee into the Offset Fund within 30 days after the end of each calendar quarter after the enactment date for which any such fee is due.

SECTION 303. BANK FINANCIAL STRENGTH.

(a) RATINGS – From time to time, but at least annually, the Director shall employ the services of two entities effectively recognized by the Division of Market Regulation of the Securities and Exchange Commission as nationally recognized statistical rating organizations for the purposes of the capital rules for broker dealers, each to conduct an assessment of the financial condition of each Bank, and of the System, for the purpose of determining the credit risk of obligations issued by each Bank and the System, including senior obligations and subordinated obligations, without regard to any connection the Bank may have to the System or that the Bank or the System may be deemed to have to the government or any form of financial backing of the Bank or the System, as the case may be, other than is provided by the financial strength of the Bank or System by itself.

(b) RATING CATEGORY – Within six months of the enactment date, each Bank shall endeavor to achieve and maintain a senior debt rating that in the opinion of both rating agencies employed pursuant to subsection (a) is equivalent to the top category or to the middle range of the second category of ratings, i.e., at least the "AA" rating, or the equivalent thereof, generally assigned by rating organizations to corporate debt. Such rating shall be made without regard to any connection that the Bank or the System may be deemed to have to the government or any form of financial backing of the Bank or the System other than is provided by the financial strength of the Bank or the System, itself.

(c) REDEMPTION OF STOCK – Effective on the [beginning date of congressional deliberations on this Act], no Bank shall permit redemption of any stock of the Bank until such time as the Bank achieves the rating prescribed by this section. Thereafter, a Bank shall not permit a redemption of stock if, in the opinion of the Director, after giving effect to the redemption of such stock, the Bank would not be in compliance with the requirements set forth in section 303(b) of this Act. Prior to permitting the redemption of any stock, the Bank shall certify to the Director that such redemption will be made in compliance with this section and shall provide copies of all calculations needed to make such certification.

(d) TRANSFERS – A Bank shall not transfer or dividend any property, including real, personal, intellectual, and any other form of property, or any form of asset, including financial assets, to the holding company created pursuant to section 304 of this Act if such transfer would cause the rating category of the Bank to fall below the rating prescribed by this section. If, at any time after the reorganization effective date, the Bank fails to achieve such rating, the holding company within 90 days shall transfer to the Bank additional capital in such amounts as are necessary to ensure that the Bank again complies with the requirements of this section.

SECTION 304. REORGANIZATION THROUGH THE FORMATION OF A HOLDING COMPANY.

(a) ACTIONS BY BANK'S BOARD OF DIRECTORS – The board of directors of each Bank may take or cause to be taken all such action as the board of directors deems necessary or appropriate to effect, upon the shareholder approval described in subsection (b) of this section, a reorganization of the ownership of the Bank, such that a holding company shall acquire full record and beneficial ownership of all of the outstanding common shares of the Bank, and the shareholders of record of the Bank on the record date chosen by the board of directors shall become the shareholders of the holding company.

(b) SHAREHOLDER APPROVAL – The plan of reorganization adopted by the board of directors pursuant to subsection (a) of this section shall be submitted to common shareholders of the Bank for their approval. The reorganization shall occur on the reorganization effective date, provided that such reorganization has been approved by the affirmative votes, cast in person or by proxy, of the holders of a majority of the issued and outstanding shares of the Bank's common stock.

(c) CERTIFICATION AND TRANSITION – Before the holding company may engage in any business activities, the Director shall certify that the Bank has achieved and maintains the rating category required by section 303 of this Act. In the event the Director makes the necessary certification and shareholders of the Bank approve the plan of reorganization under subsection (b) of this section, the following provisions shall apply beginning on the reorganization effective date:

(1) In general – Except as otherwise provided in this Act, and until the dissolution date, the Bank shall continue to have all of the rights, privileges, and obligations set forth in, and shall be subject to all of the limitations and restrictions of, the Federal Home Loan Bank Act, and, to the extent authorized by this Act, the Bank shall continue to carry out the purposes of such Act. Neither the holding company nor any subsidiary of the holding company (other than the Bank) shall be entitled to any of the rights and privileges, nor subject to the obligations, limitations, and restrictions, applicable to the Bank under the Federal Home Loan Bank Act, except as specifically provided in this Act.

(2) Transfer of certain property

(A) In general – Except as provided in this section, and with approval of the Director, on the reorganization effective date or as soon as practicable thereafter, the Bank may transfer or dividend to the holding company all real and personal property of the enterprise (both tangible and intangible) other than the remaining property; provided, however, that no such transfer or dividend, or all such transfers or dividends in the aggregate, shall in the opinion of the Director impair the ability of the Bank to maintain an AA-equivalent rating as provided in Section 303(b).

(B) Construction – Nothing in this paragraph shall be construed to prohibit the Bank from transferring remaining property from time to time to the holding company or any subsidiary of the holding company, subject to the provisions of paragraph (4).

(3) Transfer of personnel – On the reorganization effective date, employees of the Bank shall become employees of the holding company (or any subsidiary of the holding company), and the holding company (or any subsidiary of the holding company) shall provide all necessary and appropriate management and operational support to the Bank, as requested by the Bank. The Bank, however, may obtain such management and operational support from persons or entities not associated with the holding company. The holding company shall pay the salaries and other compensation for all employees of the holding company, including those from time to time assigned to assist the Bank.

(4) Dividends – The Bank may pay dividends in the form of cash or noncash distributions so long as, in the opinion of the Director, after giving effect to the payment of such dividends, the Bank would be in compliance with the requirements set forth in section 303(b) of this Act.

(5) Certification prior to dividend – Prior to the payment of any dividend under paragraph (4), the Bank shall certify to the Director that the payment of the dividend will be made in compliance with

paragraph (4) and shall provide copies of all calculations needed to make such certification.

(d) SEPARATE OPERATION –

(1) In general – The funds and assets of the Bank shall at all times be maintained separately from the funds and assets of the holding company or any subsidiary of the holding company and may be used by the Bank solely to carry out the Bank's purposes and to fulfill the Bank's obligations.

(2) Books and records – The Bank shall maintain books and records that clearly reflect the assets and liabilities of the enterprise, separate from the assets and liabilities of the holding company or any subsidiary of the holding company.

(3) Corporate office – The Bank shall maintain a corporate office that is physically separate from any office of the holding company or any subsidiary of the holding company.

(4) One officer requirement – At least one officer of the Bank shall be an officer solely of the Bank.

(5) Credit prohibition – The Bank shall not extend credit to the holding company or any subsidiary of the holding company nor guarantee or provide any credit enhancement to any debt obligations of the holding company or any subsidiary of the holding company.

(6) Amounts collected – Any amounts collected on behalf of the Bank by the holding company or any subsidiary of the holding company with respect to the assets of the Bank, pursuant to a servicing contract or other arrangement between the Bank and the holding company or any subsidiary of the holding company, shall be collected solely for the benefit of the Bank and shall be immediately deposited by the holding company or such subsidiary to an account under the sole control of the Bank.

(f) DIRECTORS –

(1) Subsection 7(a) of the Federal Home Loan Bank Act (12 U.S.C. 1427(a)) is amended—

(A) in the first sentence, by striking "eight of whom shall be elected by the members as hereinafter provided in this section and six of whom shall be appointed by the Board referred to in section 1422a of this title" and inserting "who shall be elected by the members as hereinafter provided in this section"; and

(B) by striking everything after the word "district" the second time that it appears.

(2) Paragraph 7(f)(2) of the Federal Home Loan Bank Act (12 U.S.C. 1427 (f)(2)) is amended by striking it in its entirety and renumbering the subsequent paragraphs accordingly.

(3) The amendments made by paragraphs (1) and (2) shall not apply to any appointed position of the board of directors of a Bank until the expiration of the annual term for such position during which the enactment date occurs.

(4) No director of the Bank who is appointed as a public interest director pursuant to the Federal Home Loan Bank Act may serve at the same time as a director of the holding company.

(f) ENCUMBRANCE OF ASSETS – Notwithstanding any Federal or State law, rule, or regulation, or legal or equitable principle, doctrine, or theory to the contrary, under no circumstances shall the assets of the Bank be available or used to pay claims or debts of or incurred by the holding company. Nothing in this section shall be construed to limit the right of the Bank to pay dividends not otherwise prohibited under this section.

(g) HOLDING COMPANY ACTIVITIES – After the reorganization effective date and prior to the dissolution date, all business activities of the holding company shall be conducted through subsidiaries of the holding company.

(h) RESTRICTIONS ON TRANSFER OF BANK SHARES AND BANK-RUPTCY OF THE BANK – After the reorganization effective date, the holding company shall not sell, pledge, or otherwise transfer the outstanding shares of the Bank, or agree to or cause the liquidation of the Bank or cause the Bank to file a petition for bankruptcy or insolvency, without prior approval of the Director.

(i) MERGER OR CONSOLIDATION OF BANKS – At any time prior to the dissolution date, separate Banks may merge or consolidate, provided that (1) such merger or consolidation is approved by the boards of directors of each Bank, and (2) the Director certifies that the Bank created as a result of such merger or consolidation meets the requirements of section 303 of this Act.

(j) OPERATING THE HOLDING COMPANY –

(1) Board of directors of the holding company – The number of members and composition of the board of directors of the holding company shall be determined as set forth in the holding company's charter or like instrument (as amended from time to time) or bylaws (as amended from time to time) and as permitted under the laws of the jurisdiction of the holding company's incorporation.

(2) Holding company name – The names of the holding company and any subsidiary of the holding company (other than the Bank) may not contain the name "Federal Home Loan Bank" or "bank," or any form of words implying a connection to the United States government.

(3) Disclosure required – Until five years after the dissolution date, the holding company, and any subsidiary of the holding company (other than the Bank), shall prominently display –

(A) in any document offering the holding company's securities, a statement that (1) the obligations of the holding company and any subsidiary of the holding company are not guaranteed by the full faith and credit of the United States, and (2) the holding company is not a government-sponsored enterprise of the United States; and

(B) in any advertisement or promotional materials which use the "Federal Home Loan Bank" name or mark, a statement that neither the holding company nor any subsidiary of the holding company is a government-sponsored enterprise or instrumentality of the United States.

(k) STRICT CONSTRUCTION; RIGHT TO ENFORCE

(1) Strict construction – Except as specifically set forth in this section, nothing in this section shall be construed to limit the authority of a Bank as a federally chartered organization, or of a holding company as a State or District of Columbia chartered corporation.

(2) Right to enforce – The Secretary of the Treasury or the Director, as appropriate, may request that the Attorney General bring an action in the United States District Court for the District of Columbia for the enforcement of any provision of this section, or may directly bring such an action. Such court shall have jurisdiction and power to order and require compliance with this section, to seek injunctive relief and to impose civil money penalties on the Banks, the System, the holding companies, and their officers and directors for willful failure to comply with the provisions of this Act.

SECTION 305. SUNSET.

(a) DISSOLUTION OF THE BANKS AND THE SYSTEM –

(1) The Banks – Each Bank shall dissolve, and the Bank's separate existence shall terminate on the fifth anniversary of the date of

enactment of this Act, after discharge of all outstanding debt obligations and liquidation pursuant to this subsection. The Bank may dissolve pursuant to this subsection prior to such date by notifying the Director of the Bank's intention to dissolve, and upon the Director's determination that all necessary steps to protect creditors or others have been or will be taken prior to such dissolution. On or before the dissolution date, except in cases of dissolution as a result of consolidation or merger pursuant to this Act, the Bank shall take the following actions:

> (A) Establishment of a trust for consolidated obligations – Not later than the fifth anniversary of the enactment date, each Bank shall, under the terms of one or more irrevocable trust agreements that are in form and substance satisfactory to the Secretary of the Treasury and the appointed trustee or trustees, irrevocably transfer all remaining consolidated obligations that the Secretary determines the System has issued with respect to the Bank to the trust or trusts and irrevocably deposit or cause to be deposited into such trust or trusts, to be held as trust funds solely for the benefit of holders of the remaining consolidated obligations, money or direct noncallable obligations of the United States or any agency thereof for which payment the full faith and credit of the United States is pledged, maturing as to principal and interest in such amounts and at such times as are determined by the Secretary of the Treasury to be sufficient, without consideration of any significant reinvestment of such interest, to pay the principal of, and interest on, the remaining consolidated obligations in accordance with their terms. To the extent the Bank cannot provide money or qualifying obligations in the amount required, and if the Bank has created a holding company that operates pursuant to this Act, the holding company shall be required to transfer money or qualifying obligations to the trust or trusts in the amount necessary to prevent any deficiency. All money, obligations, or financial assets deposited

into the trust or trusts pursuant to this subsection shall be applied by the trustee or trustees to the payment of the remaining consolidated obligations assumed by the trust.

(B) Obligations not transferred to the trusts – The Bank shall make proper provision for all other obligations of the Bank not transferred to the trust or trusts, including the repurchase or redemption, or the making of proper provision for the repurchase or redemption, of any preferred stock of the Bank outstanding. If the Bank has created a holding company that operates pursuant to this Act, any obligations of the Bank which cannot be fully satisfied shall become liabilities of the holding company as of the date of dissolution.

(C) Transfer of remaining assets – After compliance with this section, and if the Bank has created a holding company that operates pursuant to this Act, any remaining assets of the trust shall be transferred to the holding company or any subsidiary of the holding company, as directed by the holding company. In the event that a Bank has not created a holding company that operates pursuant to this Act, the Bank shall liquidate its remaining assets, satisfy all remaining obligations of the Bank that have not otherwise been provided for, and transfer the net proceeds of such liquidation to its shareholders on a pro rata basis.

(2) The System – The System shall dissolve and the System's separate existence shall terminate when the last Bank has been dissolved. The System shall liquidate its remaining assets, satisfy all remaining obligations of the System that have not otherwise been provided for, and transfer the net proceeds of such liquidation to the holding companies operating pursuant to section 304 on an equitable basis as shall determined by the Director in the Director's sole discretion.

(b) REPEAL OF THE FEDERAL HOME LOAN BANK ACT AND THE BANK CHARTERS THEREUNDER – On the dissolution date of each Bank, its charter shall be null and void. On the dissolution date of the System, the Federal Home Loan Bank Act shall be null and void except with respect to rights and obligations of any holders of outstanding consolidated obligations.

(c) AFFORDABLE HOUSING FUND – Before the dissolution date of the System, the Director shall cause the dissolution of the Affordable Housing Reserve Fund created pursuant to the Federal Home Loan Bank Act and the establishment of an independent not-for-profit corporation chartered under the laws of the District of Columbia to carry out the purpose of providing financial assistance for affordable housing, and shall transfer or cause to be transferred to the new corporation all funds and other property held by or for the Affordable Housing Reserve Fund. To the extent practicable, the Director shall request each holding company created under Title III of this Act to select one representative to be a director of the not-for-profit corporation. The Director shall select additional qualified persons to be directors to the extent that this is necessary to provide for a board of directors consisting of an odd number of persons who shall be at least five in number.

SECTION 2. SHORT TITLE AND TABLE OF CONTENTS.

(a) SHORT TITLE – This title may be cited as the Mortgage Holding Subsidiary Act.

(b) TABLE OF CONTENTS – The table of contents for this Act is as follows:

TITLE IV—AUTHORIZATION FOR INSURED DEPOSITORY INSTITUTIONS AND HOLDING COMPANIES TO OWN OR CONTROL MORTGAGE HOLDING SUBSIDIARIES

SECTION 401. DEFINITIONS.

For the purposes of this title, the following definitions shall apply:

(1) Appropriate Federal banking agency. The term "appropriate Federal banking agency" is defined in section 3(q) of the Federal Deposit Insurance Act (12 U.S.C. 1813(q)).

(2) Federal banking agency. The term "Federal banking agency" is defined in section 3(z) of the Federal Deposit Insurance Act (12 U.S.C. 1813(z)).

(3) Holding company. The term "holding company" means a "bank holding company," as that term is defined in section 2(a) of the Bank Holding Company Act (12 U.S.C. 1841(a)) and a "financial holding company," as that term is defined in 2(p) of the Bank Holding Company Act (12 U.S.C. 1841(p)).

(4) Insured credit union. The term "insured credit union" is defined in section 101(7) of the Federal Credit Union Act (12 U.S.C. 1752(7)).

(5) Insured depository institution. The term "insured depository institution" is defined in section 3(c)(2) of the Federal Deposit Insurance Act (12 U.S.C. 1813(c)(2)).

(6) Mortgage. The term "mortgage" means a recorded lien or deed of trust on real estate, securing an obligation of a holder of an interest in real estate, whether or not that lien is senior to other liens on that real estate. The term "mortgage" shall include the obligation it secures.

(7) Mortgage holding subsidiary. The term "mortgage holding subsidiary" means a for-profit, general business corporation, chartered by a State, that is formed for the purpose of owning, servicing, or securitizing mortgages on residential properties.

(8) Mortgage holding subsidiary parent. The term "mortgage holding subsidiary parent" means an "insured depository institution" and a "holding company," as those terms are defined in this section.

(9) Residential property. The term "residential property" includes owner-occupied, renter-occupied, or other structures housing natural persons, including mixed-use properties where the residential component of the property constitutes at least 75 percent of the value of the property, excluding the value of the land underlying the structure or structures.

(10) Securitizing mortgages. The term "securitizing mortgages" encompasses—

(A) the sale or other transfer of a pool of mortgages to a third-party trust which in turn issues and sells securities or other undivided beneficial interests in the payments of principal and interest on such pooled mortgages; and

(B) in-situ securitization whereby the mortgage holding subsidiary, or a subsidiary of the subsidiary, may finance its interest in a pool of mortgages of which it retains record and beneficial ownership by granting a security interest in such pool in favor of a funding source and guaranteeing to such funding source the timely payment of principal and interest on the mortgages in such pool.

(11) State. The term "State" is defined in section 3(a)(3) of the Federal Deposit Insurance Act (12 U.S.C. 1813(a)(3)).

(12) Well capitalized and adequately capitalized. The terms "well capitalized" and "adequately capitalized" are defined in section 38 of the Federal Deposit Insurance Act (12 U.S.C. 1831o).

SECTION 402. MORTGAGE HOLDING SUBSIDIARY.

(a) MORTGAGE HOLDING SUBSIDIARY AUTHORIZED – A mortgage holding subsidiary parent may own, control, or hold an equity interest in one or more mortgage holding subsidiaries.

(b) PERMITTED ACTIVITIES – A mortgage holding subsidiary may—

(1) share directors, officers, employees, and facilities with any party that owns, controls, or holds an equity interest in the mortgage holding subsidiary;

(2) purchase mortgages from mortgage originators, including its mortgage holding subsidiary parent or parents, or in the secondary mortgage market, provided that such mortgages are liens on real estate located within one or more States;

(3) issue debt and guarantees which have a preference in conservatorship, receivership, liquidation, or under Title 11 of the U.S. Code over other unsecured debt, guarantees, and obligations of the subsidiary, except as provided in paragraph 403(a)(3) of this title; and

(4) finance the mortgages in which it holds the record and beneficial interest by granting a security interest in a pool of such mortgages and guaranteeing the timely payment of principal and interest on such pooled mortgages.

(c) PROHIBITED ACTIVITIES – A mortgage holding subsidiary may not—

(1) directly or indirectly engage in any activity as an equity capital participant, other than activities directly related to owning, servicing, or securitizing mortgages on residential real estate;

(2) accept deposits, as that term is defined in section 1813(l) of this title, or accept an obligation, payable outside any State, that would be a deposit if it were carried on the books and records of a depository institution and would be payable at an office located in a State;

(3) sell debt of the mortgage holding subsidiary to a natural person in an amount less than $100,000; or

(4) take any action which suggests to the general public or to holders of its debt that such debt or guarantees or other obligations are in any manner guaranteed or otherwise protected against loss of principal or interest by a mortgage holding subsidiary parent, an insured credit union, the Federal Deposit Insurance Corporation, or the National Credit Union Share Insurance Fund.

(d) MORTGAGE HOLDING SUBSIDIARY NOT SUBJECT TO BANK, THRIFT, OR HOLDING COMPANY REGULATION – A mortgage holding subsidiary owned or controlled by a mortgage holding subsidiary parent shall not be subject to supervision or regulation by the appropriate Federal banking agency of such parent, except as provided in this section, or to supervision or regulation by any other Federal banking agency.

(e) APPLICABILITY OF FEDERAL AND STATE LAWS – A mortgage holding subsidiary shall be subject to all Federal and State laws applicable to state-chartered business corporations.

SECTION 403. SAFEGUARDS FOR THE MORTGAGE HOLDING SUBSIDIARY PARENT.

(a) A MORTGAGE HOLDING SUBSIDIARY PARENT, WITH REGARD TO A MORTGAGE HOLDING SUBSIDIARY THE PARENT OWNS OR CONTROLS, MAY NOT –

(1) engage in any transaction with a mortgage holding subsidiary that would be impermissible under sections 23A and 23B of the Federal Reserve Act (12 U.S.C. 371c and 12 U.S.C. 371c-1);

(2) guarantee any debt or other liability or obligation of a mortgage holding subsidiary; or

(3) make an equity or subordinated debt investment in a mortgage holding subsidiary if, immediately after making such investment, the mortgage holding subsidiary parent shall be less than well capitalized, after taking into account section 404 of this title. If the mortgage holding subsidiary parent, immediately after making an investment in a mortgage holding subsidiary, is less than well capitalized, the appropriate Federal banking agency shall direct the subsidiary to return a sufficient amount of that investment to the parent to restore the parent to the status of being well capitalized. Until such time as a sufficient amount of the investment is returned to the mortgage holding subsidiary parent, the

appropriate Federal banking agency shall have a claim on unsecured assets of the mortgage holding subsidiary superior to all other unsecured claims on the subsidiary. The claim shall bear interest, equal to the ninety-one-day Treasury bill rate plus six percent, until the claim is paid. Should a mortgage holding subsidiary become a debtor under Title 11 of the U.S. Code, any claim by the appropriate Federal banking agency under this paragraph, including accrued but unpaid interest, shall become immediately due and payable.

(b) INDEMNIFICATION OF A MORTGAGE HOLDING SUBSIDIARY PARENT ARISING FROM THE ACTIVITIES OF A MORTGAGE HOLDING SUBSIDIARY – A mortgage holding subsidiary shall indemnify its mortgage holding subsidiary parent or parents against any judgments against the parent or parents arising out of the actions of the subsidiary.

(c) AUTHORITY OF THE APPROPRIATE FEDERAL BANKING AGENCY –

(1) The appropriate Federal banking agency shall have the right to examine the assets, liabilities, and operations of a mortgage holding subsidiary, but only to determine the degree to which the subsidiary poses a threat to the safe and sound condition or solvency of the mortgage holding subsidiary parent or parents which own or control the subsidiary or is in violation of any provision in subsection (a) of this section.

(2) The appropriate Federal banking agency, after giving notice and holding a public hearing, may direct a mortgage holding subsidiary parent to take such actions as are feasible to strengthen the balance sheet and operations of the mortgage holding subsidiary or, if such actions are not feasible, to divest all or a portion of any equity interest the parent may have in the subsidiary, after determining that continued ownership or control of the subsidiary by the parent could be so detrimental to the safe and sound

operation of the parent as to materially increase the likelihood that the parent may become less than adequately capitalized.

(3) The appropriate Federal banking agency shall have the right to use the powers granted to it under this title to enforce against the violation of any provision in subsection (a) of this section.

SECTION 404. CAPITAL DEDUCTION.

(a) CAPITAL DEDUCTION REQUIRED – In determining compliance with applicable capital standards –

(1) the aggregate amount of the outstanding subordinated debt and equity investment, including retained earnings, of a mortgage holding subsidiary parent in all mortgage holding subsidiaries shall be deducted from the assets, tangible equity, and subordinated debt of the mortgage holding subsidiary parent; and

(2) the assets and liabilities of the mortgage holding subsidiaries shall not be consolidated, for regulatory capital purposes, with those of the mortgage holding subsidiary parent.

(b) FINANCIAL STATEMENT DISCLOSURE OF CAPITAL DEDUCTION – Any published financial statement of a mortgage holding subsidiary parent that owns or controls a mortgage holding subsidiary shall, in addition to providing information prepared in accordance with generally accepted accounting principles, separately present financial information for the parent in the manner provided in subsection (a) of this section.

SECTION 405. REGULATIONS.

Within 180 days after enactment of this section, the appropriate Federal banking agencies shall publish for comment such regulations as are needed to carry out the purposes of this title.

SECTION 406. COORDINATED EXAMINATION OF MORTGAGE HOLDING SUBSIDIARIES.

Should two or more mortgage holding subsidiary parents own or control a mortgage holding subsidiary, the Federal banking agencies with the primary federal responsibility for supervising those mortgage holding subsidiary parents shall coordinate the examination of the mortgage holding subsidiary so as to eliminate duplicative examinations of the subsidiary.

SECTION 407. CONFORMING AMENDMENTS.

(a) CAPITAL REGULATION –

(1) Federal Deposit Insurance Act.— Section 38(b)(2)(F) of the Federal Deposit Insurance Act (12 U.S.C. 1831o(b)(2)(F)) is amended at the end by adding the following: ", provided that the term 'relevant capital measure' excludes in all cases in which it is applied the assets, liabilities, and capital of all mortgage holding subsidiaries (as defined in subsection 401(7) of the Mortgage Holding Subsidiary Act) owned or controlled by an insured depository institution."

(2) Bank Holding Company Act.— Section 5(b) of the Bank Holding Company Act (12 U.S.C. 1844(b)) is amended at the end by adding the following: ", provided that in administering its capital adequacy regulations for bank holding companies, financial holding companies, and State member banks (as defined in section 1813(d)(2) of this title), the Board shall exclude from all capital adequacy calculations the assets, liabilities, and capital of all mortgage holding subsidiaries (as defined in subsection 401(7) of the Mortgage Holding Subsidiary Act) owned or controlled by an insured depository institution subsidiary of a bank holding company or a financial holding company."

(b) SAVINGS AND LOAN HOLDING COMPANY AMENDMENTS –

(1) Holding company activities – Section 301 of the Financial Institutions Reform, Recovery, and Enforcement Act of 1989, amending the Home Owners' Loan Act (12 U.S.C. 1461 et seq.), is amended in Sec. 10(c)(1) (12 U.S.C. 1467a(c)(1)) by inserting after "association": ", except a mortgage holding subsidiary (as defined in subsection 401(7) of the Mortgage Holding Subsidiary Act),."

(2) Qualified thrift lender test – Sec. 303(a) of the Financial Institutions Reform, Recovery, and Enforcement Act of 1989, amending the Home Owners' Loan Act (12 U.S.C. 1461 et seq.), is amended in Sec. 10(m)(4)(C) (12 U.S.C. 1467a(m)(4)(C)) by adding at the end the following new clause:

"(vi) Mortgage holding subsidiaries – For the purposes of this subparagraph the term "qualified thrift investments" shall include the assets of any mortgage holding subsidiary (as defined in subsection 401(7) of the Mortgage Holding Subsidiary Act) owned or controlled by a savings association as if those assets were assets owned by the savings association, provided that if the savings association owns less than 100 percent of the voting stock of a mortgage holding subsidiary, the assets of the subsidiary shall be treated as assets of the savings association in proportion to the percentage of the voting stock of the subsidiary owned by the association."

(c) REAL ESTATE APPRAISALS – Section 1121(4) of the Financial Institutions Reform, Recovery, and Enforcement Act of 1989 (12 U.S.C. 3350(4)), is amended by redesignating the paragraph as subparagraph (A) and adding the following new subparagraph:

"(B) A federally related transaction shall not mean a real estate related financial transaction where the financial institution originating the transaction intends that the product of the transaction will be sold to a mortgage holding subsidiary (as defined in subsection 401(7) of the Mortgage Holding Subsidiary Act) owned or controlled by the financial institution and in fact executes that sale in a timely manner."

(d) COMMUNITY REINVESTMENT ACT – Section 803(2) of the Community Reinvestment Act of 1977 (12 U.S.C. 2902(2)) is amended at the end by adding the following: ", excluding a mortgage holding subsidiary (as defined in subsection 401(7) of the Mortgage Holding Subsidiary Act) owned or controlled by an insured depository institution."

(e) TYING ARRANGEMENTS –

(1) Bank Holding Company Act Amendments of 1970 – Section 106(a) of the Bank Holding Company Act Amendments of 1970 (12 U.S.C. 1971) is amended by adding at the end the following: "For purposes of this chapter, transactions between a bank, a customer of the bank, and a mortgage holding subsidiary (as defined in subsection 401(7) of the Mortgage Holding Subsidiary Act) owned or controlled by the bank shall be exempt from the provisions of this chapter."

(2) Home Owners' Loan Act – Section 301 of the Financial Institutions Reform, Recovery, and Enforcement Act of 1989, in amending section 5(q) of the Home Owners' Loan Act (12 U.S.C. 1464(q)), is amended by adding at the end the following paragraph:

"(7) For purposes of this subsection, transactions between a savings association, a customer of the savings association, and a mortgage holding subsidiary (as defined in subsection 401(7) of the Mortgage Holding Subsidiary Act) owned or controlled by the savings association shall be exempt from the provisions of this subsection."

Appendixes

Appendix 1

TABLE A-1

CAPITAL HELD BY THE GSES AND TEN OF THE LARGEST
U.S. FINANCIAL INSTITUTIONS (in thousands of dollars)

Companies Ranked by Assets	Balance Sheet Assets	Stockholder's Equity	Capital Ratio: Equity to Assets
Citigroup Inc.	$1,097,190	$86,718	7.9%
Fannie Mae	$887,515	$16,288	1.8%
Federal Home Loan Bank System	$763,631	$36,324	4.8%
JP Morgan Chase & Co	$758,800	$42,306	5.6%
Freddie Mac	$752,249	$31,330	4.2%
Bank of America Corp	$660,458	$50,319	7.6%
Wells Fargo & Co	$349,259	$30,358	8.7%
Wachovia Corp	$341,839	$32,078	9.4%
Bank One Corp	$277,383	$22,440	8.1%
Washington Mutual Inc.	$268,298	$20,134	7.5%
FleetBoston Financial Corp	$190,453	$16,833	8.8%
US Bancorp	$180,027	$18,101	10.1%
American Express Co	$157,253	$13,861	8.8%
Average all companies	—	—	7.2%
Average GSEs	—	—	3.6%
Average excluding GSEs	—	—	8.2%

SOURCE: Office of Management and Budget, "Credit and Insurance," chapter 7 in *Analytical Perspectives, Budget of the United States Government, Fiscal Year* 2005 (Washington, D.C.: U.S. Government Printing Office, 2004), 84.

Appendix 2

TABLE A-2

ESTIMATES OF THE JUMBO AND NONJUMBO MORTGAGE RATE DIFFERENTIAL

Study	Time Period	Regions
Hendershott and Shilling (1989)	May–July 1986	California
ICF (1990)	May–July 1987 April–September 1987	California Illinois New Jersey 7 states
Cotterman and Pearce (1996)	Quarterly 1989–1993	California 11 states
Pearce (2000)	Quarterly 1992–1999	California 11 states

Data Screens	Results
Fixed rate Thrifts only No construction or purchase loans Term $\geq$ 25 years LTV $\geq$ 70% No buydowns	Contract rate 24 to 34 basis points Effective rate 29 to 39 basis points
Same as Hendershott and Shilling Effective rate $\geq$ 7.5% LTV $\leq$ 100%	Six-month sample, 7 states, 23 California, 26 basis points

Fixed rate
Term $\geq$ 25 years
No buydowns
LTV $\geq$ 70%
LTV $\leq$ 100%
Points $\leq$ 15% or $30,000
Effective rate $\geq$ 75th percentile of the effective
  rate on ARMs for the month
Effective rate $\leq$ 2.05%above the monthly
  Ginnie Mae yield
Loan amounts between $35,000 and $450,000
Thrifts and mortgage companies
Used MIRS sample weights
	25 to 50 basis points for California
	
	24 to 60 basis points for the 11 states

Fixed rate
Term = 30 years
No buydowns
LTV $\geq$ 70%
LTV $\leq$ 90%
Points $\leq$ 9% or $30,000
Effective rate $\geq$ 75th percentile of the effective rate
  on ARMs for the month
Effective rate $\leq$ 1.1% above the monthly
  Freddie Mac survey yield
Loan amounts between 20% and 200% of the
  conforming loan limit
Thrifts and mortgage companies
Does not use MIRS sample weights
	California averaged 27 basis points
	11 states averaged 24 basis points

(continued on following page)

(Table A-2 *continued*)

Estimates of the Jumbo and Nonjumbo Mortgage Rate Differential

Study	Time Period	Regions
Ambrose, Buttimer, and Thibodeau (2001)	May–July of 1990–1999	Dallas
Naranjo and Toevs (2002)	1986–1998	No screen
Passmore, Sparks, and Ingpen (2002)	1992–1999	California
U.S. Congressional Budget Office (2001)	1995:Q1 to 2000:Q2	No screen
McKenzie (2002)	1986–2000	No screen

STUDIES: B. W. Ambrose, R. Buttimer, and T. Thibodeau, "A New Spin on the Jumbo/Conforming Loan Rate Differential," *Journal of Real Estate Finance and Economics* 23 (2001): 309–35; R. F. Cotterman and J. E. Pearce, "The Effect of the Federal National Mortgage Association and the Federal Home Loan Mortgage Corporation on Conventional Fixed-Rate Mortgage Yields," *Studies on Privatizing Fannie Mae and Freddie Mac* (U.S. Department of Housing and Urban Development, Office of Policy Development and Research, 1996); P. H. Hendershott and J. Shilling, "The Impact of the Agencies on Conventional Fixed-Rate Mortgage Yields," *Journal of Real Estate Finance and Economics* 2 (1989): 101–15; ICF Incorporated, "Effects of the Conforming Loan Limit on Mortgage Markets," Report prepared for the U.S. Department of Housing and Urban Development, *Office of Policy Development and Research,* 1990; J. A. McKenzie, "A

Data Screens	Results
Update of Cotterman and Pearce	24 basis points without adjustment for house price volatility 16 basis points after adjusting for house price volatility
Fixed rate Term ≥ 25 years LTV ≥ 70% LTV ≤ 100% Fees ≤ 15% or $30,000 Delete top and bottom 5% based on effective interest rate Exclude commercial bank mortgages	8 basis points (1994) to 43 basis points (1989)
Fixed rate Term = 30 years LTV ≤ 80% Principal ≥ $125,000 Rate 5% to 12% Jumbo loans at least $20,000 above but less than twice the conforming loan limit	18 to 23 basis points
LTV ≥ 20% and LTV ≤ 97% Principal between 25% and 200% of the conforming loan limit	4 to 35 basis points Average 22.8 basis points
Fixed rate Existing properties Term = 30 years Loan balances within a 75% tolerance around the conforming loan limit Excludes loans with a rate more than 50 basis points below or more than 200 basis points above the monthly median rate	Range of annual estimates is from 10 basis points (1994) to 35 basis points (1989) Average is 22 basis points over the 1986–2000 period Average is 19 basis points over the 1996–2000 period

Reconsideration of the Jumbo/Non-Jumbo Mortgage Rate Differential," *Journal of Real Estate Finance and Economics* 25 (2002): 197–213; A. Naranjo and A. Toevs, "The Effects of Purchases of Mortgages and Securitization by Government-Sponsored Enterprises on Mortgage Yield Spreads and Volatility," *Journal of Real Estate Finance and Economics* 25 (2002): 173–96; W. Passmore, R. Sparks, and J. Ingpen. "GSEs, Mortgage Rates, and the Long-Run Effects of Mortgage Securitization," *Journal of Real Estate Finance and Economics* 25 (2002): 215–42; J. E. Pearce, "Conforming Loan Differentials: 1992–1999," Welch Consulting, College Station, Tex., 2000 (unpublished); U.S. Congressional Budget Office, "Interest Rate Differentials between Jumbo and Conforming Mortgages," 2001.

Appendix 3. Industrial AA-Agencies, Smoothed Data, January 3, 1994, to January 1, 2004

FIGURE A-1
AT THREE YEARS

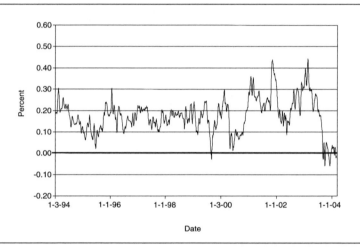

SOURCE: Bloomberg, L.P. website.

FIGURE A-2
AT FIVE YEARS

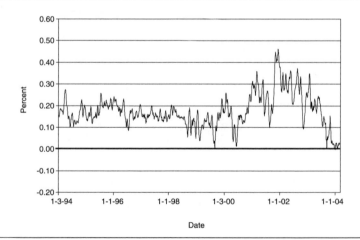

SOURCE: Bloomberg, L.P. website.

FIGURE A-3
AT SEVEN YEARS

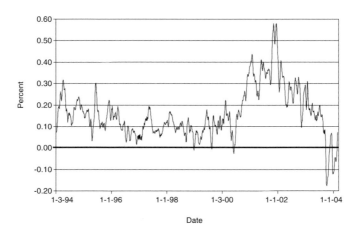

SOURCE: Bloomberg, L.P. website.

FIGURE A-4
AT TEN YEARS

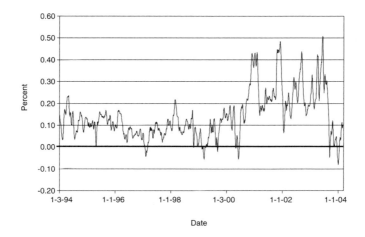

SOURCE: Bloomberg, L.P. website.

Notes

1. A recent Federal Reserve staff paper makes exactly this point with respect to Fannie and Freddie—that they create serious risks for the government but contribute only marginally to the financing of housing. See Wayne Passmore, "The GSE Implicit Subsidy and Value of Government Ambiguity," December 22, 2003 (preliminary draft).

2. These links and benefits include the following: The president is authorized to appoint five members of their eighteen-member boards of directors (although the Bush administration has chosen not to make any appointments since 2003); they are exempt from state and local income taxes; the secretary of the Treasury is authorized to invest up to $2.25 billion in the securities of each GSE; their securities are eligible collateral for U.S. funds held in banks; and banks and other federally regulated depository institutions may invest in Fannie and Freddie securities without prudential limit.

3. The total principal amount of Fannie and Freddie's direct obligations outstanding is difficult to pin down because of the unavailability for more than a year of financial information from Freddie Mac. In this memorandum we use the numbers in a paper issued by the FDIC on March 1, 2004, *Assessing the Banking Industry's Exposure to an Implicit Government Guarantee of the GSEs.*

4. Alan Greenspan, prepared statement before Committee on Banking, Housing and Urban Affairs, United States Senate, 108th Cong., 1st sess., February 24, 2004, 7–8.

5. Franklin Raines, remarks prepared for delivery before the American Enterprise Institute, February 6, 2004, www.Fanniemae.com/speeches/printthis page.jhtml?repID=media/speeches/20.

6. Greenspan, prepared statement before Committee on Banking, Housing and Urban Affairs, 6–7.

7. See, e.g., letter of January 31, 2001, from Thomas J. McCool and Lynn H. Gibson of the General Accounting Office to Chairman Richard H. Baker, detailing the differences between the authorities of bank regulators and those of OFHEO. GAO-01-322R *Financial Regulators' Enforcement Authorities.*

8. According to the FDIC, holdings of GSE-related securities, including indirect obligations of Fannie and Freddie and MBSs guaranteed by Fannie and

Freddie, amount to 154.6 percent of the combined Tier 1 capital of commercial banks and savings associations. In the case of Fannie and Freddie direct obligations, the totals are 45.5 percent of Tier 1 capital for commercial banks and 26.8 percent for savings associations. In the case of MBSs, the totals are 153.8 percent for commercial banks and 105.6 percent for savings associations. FDIC, *Assessing the Banking Industry's Exposure to an Implicit Government Guarantee of the GSEs.*

9. Office of Federal Housing Enterprise Oversight, *Systemic Risk: Fannie Mae, Freddie Mac and the Role of OFHEO*, report, February 2003.

10. OFHEO Report, 98.

11. Theoretically, the Fed could purchase Fannie or Freddie debt and thus restore its value, but this would be a very risky proposition and highly unlikely. One reason it is risky is that, as noted already, there is no legal mechanism for shutting down the financially troubled or insolvent GSE. The Fed could restore the GSE's market credibility but could take significant losses if the GSE continues to operate and incurs additional losses. In addition, Congress may ultimately decide not to bail out all creditors, and this might especially be true if the Fed's purchases have calmed the market sufficiently so that the crisis is past. Normally, when the Fed floods the market with liquidity in a financial crisis, it purchases riskless U.S. Treasury securities. There is no legal assurance that the holders of Fannie or Freddie securities will be bailed out and thus no assurance that the Fed will be reimbursed for its losses. In any case, whether or not the Fed is reimbursed, these would be taxpayer losses.

12. OFHEO Report, 92 (footnote omitted).

13. Raines speech to Merrill Lynch Investor Conference, September 14, 1999.

14. For a discussion of this process, see Peter Wallison and Bert Ely, *Nationalizing Mortgage Risk: The Growth of Fannie Mae and Freddie Mac* (Washington, D.C.: AEI Press, 2000).

15. Greenspan, prepared statement before Committee on Banking, Housing and Urban Affairs.

16. Congressional Budget Office, *Federal Subsidies and the Housing GSEs* (Washington, D.C.: U.S. Government Printing Office, 2001), 33.

17. Passmore paper, op. cit., note 1.

18. David B. Gross, "The Government's Role in Promoting Financial Stability," *Fannie Mae Papers* 2, no. 3 (July 2003): 6–7.

19. Congressional Budget Office, *Federal Subsidies and the Housing GSEs*, 31.

20. Office of Management and Budget, *The President's 2005 Budget,* Analytical Perspectives, 8.

21. See, e.g., Joint Center for Housing Studies, Harvard University, *The 25th Anniversary of the Community Reinvestment Act: Access to Capital in an Evolving Financial Services System* (Cambridge, Mass.: Harvard University, March 2002), iv, 13 (institutions subject to the Community Reinvestment Act lead the primary market in serving low-income people and neighborhoods, while GSEs trail behind).

22. On June 14, 2004, Ann McLaughlin Korologos, the chair of Fannie's Corporate Governance Committee, wrote the following in a letter to OFHEO that commented on OFHEO's proposed corporate governance regulations: "[W]e are concerned that the proposal's focus on the federal charters and 'public mission' of [Fannie and Freddie] may detract from our role as representatives of Fannie Mae's shareholders. As directors, our duty is to act in the best interests of the shareholders."

23. The privatization of the FHLBs will also terminate the FHLB payments that support the Treasury's obligations with respect to the outstanding RefCorp bonds. We make no specific proposal in the Privatization Act for dealing with this question but note that extinguishing the government's obligation on the RefCorp bonds is not a sufficient reason to continue the existence of the FHLB system.

24. In his testimony to the Senate Banking Committee on February 24, 2004, Chairman Greenspan proposed placing a cap on the debt Fannie and Freddie would be permitted to issue, noting that this would reduce the risks they pose to the economy but still permit them to support the mortgage market: "One way the Congress could constrain the size of [the GSEs'] balance sheets is to alter the composition of Fannie's and Freddie's mortgage financing by limiting the dollar amount of their debt relative to the dollar amount of mortgages securitized and held by other investors. . . . [T]his approach would continue to expand the depth and liquidity of the capital markets through mortgage securitization but would remove most of the potential systemic risks associated with these GSEs." This is a salutary approach with one shortcoming: It keeps the two GSEs in their position of market dominance as a shared government-sponsored monopoly in the secondary mortgage market.

25. Franklin Raines, remarks, "Government Policy and Financial Market Stability: The Case of Fannie Mae" (conference, American Enterprise Institute, Washington, D.C., February 6, 2004).

26. Greenspan, prepared statement before Committee on Banking, Housing and Urban Affairs, 5–6.

27. The impact of bank capital requirements on the costs banks and thrifts incur in holding mortgages in portfolio is significant, which gives banks and thrifts a powerful incentive to sell mortgages rather than hold them. The MHS concept would dramatically reduce those costs and thus reduce the present bias toward selling mortgages into the secondary market. If an MHS did not assume any interest-rate risk on the mortgages it owned, it could safely operate with a 1% capital level in owning mortgages with a credit quality comparable to the quality of mortgages Fannie and Freddie own or guarantee. That percentage is 4% below the minimum leverage ratio for a well-capitalized bank or thrift and 6.3% below the weighted average leverage capital ratio of 7.3% on September 30, 2003, for the nation's 100 largest commercial banks. Assuming a 14% after-tax return on equity capital placed

at risk for home mortgage credit losses and a 39% tax rate, which produces a 23% required pretax return (0.14/(1 − 0.39)), and a 5% debt funding cost, the pretax cost differential between debt and equity capital is 18% (23% − 5%), or 18 basis points per 1% of the amount financed (18%/100). Therefore, an MHS exempt from regulatory capital requirements would operate at a 72 basis point cost advantage when compared to a bank, if we assume that the bank would be capitalized at the 5% minimum leverage ratio ((5% − 1%) × 18). That regulatory cost advantage rises to 113 basis points ((7.3% − 1%) × 18) at the average leverage ratio for large banks. Barring MHS from accepting deposits will eliminate for MHS other expenses banks incur by virtue of being federally insured and regulated depository institutions. While these cost savings have not been estimated, they undoubtedly amount to at least a few basis points per asset dollar.

28. Although the funding costs of AA-rated banks are somewhat higher than industrial AA credits, Ely believes that the stability and high quality of an MHS's portfolio would warrant its treatment for rating purposes as closer to an industrial than a bank credit.

29. "Fannie: Origination Costs up Sharply," *National Mortgage News Daily Briefly*, September 30, 2003.

30. "Fees, Fees, and More Fees," *Washington Post*, June 7, 2003, F1.

31. Mercer Oliver Wyman, "Study on the Financial Integration of European Mortgage Markets," European Mortgage Federation, October 2003.

32. By retaining the ownership of mortgages, MHS may succeed in selling borrowers on an intriguing innovation, "ratchet mortgages," which are adjustable-rate mortgages that adjust only one way: down. Ratchet mortgages would be funded by "ratchet bonds" with a matching rate adjustment feature. Ratchet mortgages funded by ratchet bonds would further lower all-in mortgage rates by (1) completely eliminating refinancing costs, (2) completely eliminating reinvestment risk for bondholders, and (3) eliminating for bondholders the cost of reinvesting prepaid funds. The latter cost has been particularly significant in recent years for MBS investors. The interest-rate payoff of ratchet bonds has not yet been estimated, but it could be significant. The Tennessee Valley Authority has issued $1.1 billion of ratchet bonds, an early indication of their market acceptance.

About the Authors

Peter J. Wallison joined AEI in 1999 as a resident fellow and the codirector of AEI's program on financial market deregulation. As a partner of Gibson, Dunn & Crutcher LLP, he practiced banking, corporate, and financial law in the firm's Washington and New York offices. As the general counsel of the Treasury Department from 1981 to 1985, Mr. Wallison helped develop the Reagan administration's proposals for deregulating the financial services industry. In 1986 and 1987, Mr. Wallison was counsel to President Ronald Reagan. He is the author of *Back from the Brink: A Practical Plan for Privatizing Deposit Insurance and Strengthening Our Banks and Thrifts* (1990); the coauthor of *Nationalizing Mortgage Risk: The Growth of Fannie Mae and Freddie Mac* (2000) and *The GAAP Gap: Corporate Disclosure in the Internet Age* (2000). He edited *Serving Two Masters, Yet Out of Control: Fannie Mae and Freddie Mac* (2001) and *Optional Federal Chartering and Regulation of Insurance Companies* (2000), all of which were published by the AEI Press. Mr. Wallison's most recent book is *Ronald Reagan: The Power of Conviction and the Success of His Presidency* (Westview Press, 2002).

Thomas H. Stanton is a Washington, D.C.–based attorney. His practice relates to the capacity of public institutions to deliver services effectively, specializing in government organization and program design, financial regulation, government corporations, government-sponsored enterprises, and privatization. Mr. Stanton is a former member of the federal senior executive service. He chairs the Standing Panel on Executive Organization and Management at the National Academy of Public Administration and is a fellow of the Center for the Study of American Government at Johns Hopkins University, where he teaches the law of public institutions. Mr. Stanton's writings include *A State of Risk* (HarperCollins, 1991),

Government-Sponsored Enterprises: Mercantilist Companies in the Modern World (AEI Press, 2002), and many articles. Mr. Stanton's most recent book, which he edited with Benjamin Ginsberg, is *Making Government Manageable* (Johns Hopkins University Press, 2004).

Bert Ely is a financial institutions and monetary policy consultant. The principal at Ely & Company, Inc., in Alexandria, Virginia, he has specialized in deposit insurance and banking-structure issues since 1981. In 1986, he was one of the first analysts to predict a taxpayer bailout of the Federal Savings and Loan Insurance Corporation. He monitors conditions in the banking and thrift industries, the politics of the credit-allocation process, and issues concerning monetary policy and the payments system.

.

Board of Trustees

Bruce Kovner, *Chairman*
Chairman
Caxton Associates, LLC

Lee R. Raymond,
Vice Chairman
Chairman and CEO
Exxon Mobil Corporation

Tully M. Friedman, *Treasurer*
Chairman and CEO
Friedman Fleischer & Lowe LLC

Gordon M. Binder
Managing Director
Coastview Capital, LLC

Harlan Crow
Chairman
Crow Holdings

Christopher DeMuth
President
American Enterprise Institute

Morton H. Fleischer
Chairman and CEO
Spirit Finance Corporation

Christopher B. Galvin
Retired Chairman and CEO
Motorola, Inc.

Raymond V. Gilmartin
Chairman, President, and CEO
Merck & Co., Inc.

Harvey Golub
Chairman and CEO, Retired
American Express Company

Robert F. Greenhill
Chairman
Greenhill & Co., LLC

Roger Hertog
Vice Chairman
Alliance Capital Management
 Corporation

Martin M. Koffel
Chairman and CEO
URS Corporation

John A. Luke Jr.
Chairman and CEO
MeadWestvaco Corporation

L. Ben Lytle
Chairman Emeritus
Anthem, Inc.

Alex J. Mandl
CEO
Gemplus International

Robert A. Pritzker
President and CEO
Colson Associates, Inc.

J. Joe Ricketts
Chairman and Founder
Ameritrade Holding Corporation

George R. Roberts
Kohlberg Kravis Roberts & Co.

The American Enterprise Institute
for Public Policy Research

Founded in 1943, AEI is a nonpartisan, nonprofit research
and educational organization based in Washington, D.C.
The Institute sponsors research, conducts seminars and
conferences, and publishes books and periodicals.

AEI's research is carried out under three major programs: Economic Policy Studies; Foreign Policy and
Defense Studies; and Social and Political Studies.
The resident scholars and fellows listed in these pages
are part of a network that also includes ninety adjunct
scholars at leading universities throughout the United
States and in several foreign countries.

The views expressed in AEI publications are those of
the authors and do not necessarily reflect the views of
the staff, advisory panels, officers, or trustees.

Kevin B. Rollins
President and CEO
Dell, Inc.

John W. Rowe
Chairman and CEO
Exelon Corporation

Edward B. Rust Jr.
Chairman and CEO
State Farm Insurance Companies

William S. Stavropoulos
Chairman and CEO
The Dow Chemical Company

Wilson H. Taylor
Chairman Emeritus
CIGNA Corporation

Marilyn Ware
Chairman Emeritus
American Water

James Q. Wilson
Pepperdine University

Emeritus Trustees

Willard C. Butcher

Richard B. Madden

Robert H. Malott

Paul W. McCracken

Paul F. Oreffice

Henry Wendt

Officers

Christopher DeMuth
President

David Gerson
Executive Vice President

Jason Bertsch
Vice President, Marketing

Montgomery B. Brown
Vice President, Publications

Danielle Pletka
Vice President, Foreign and Defense
Policy Studies

Council of Academic
Advisers

James Q. Wilson, *Chairman*
Pepperdine University

Eliot A. Cohen
Professor and Director of Strategic
 Studies
School of Advanced International
 Studies
Johns Hopkins University

Gertrude Himmelfarb
Distinguished Professor of History
 Emeritus
City University of New York

Samuel P. Huntington
Albert J. Weatherhead III
 University Professor of Government
Harvard University

William M. Landes
Clifton R. Musser Professor of Law
 and Economics
University of Chicago Law School

Sam Peltzman
Ralph and Dorothy Keller
 Distinguished Service Professor
 of Economics
University of Chicago
 Graduate School of Business

Nelson W. Polsby
Heller Professor of Political Science
Institute of Government Studies
University of California–Berkeley

George L. Priest
John M. Olin Professor of Law and
 Economics
Yale Law School

Jeremy Rabkin
Professor of Government
Cornell University

Murray L. Weidenbaum
Mallinckrodt Distinguished
 University Professor
Washington University

Richard J. Zeckhauser
Frank Plumpton Ramsey Professor
 of Political Economy
Kennedy School of Government
Harvard University

Research Staff

Gautam Adhikari
Visiting Fellow

Joseph Antos
Wilson H. Taylor Scholar in Health
 Care and Retirement Policy

Leon Aron
Resident Scholar

Claude E. Barfield
Resident Scholar; Director, Science
 and Technology Policy Studies

Roger Bate
Visiting Fellow

Walter Berns
Resident Scholar

Douglas J. Besharov
Joseph J. and Violet Jacobs
 Scholar in Social Welfare Studies

Karlyn H. Bowman
Resident Fellow

John E. Calfee
Resident Scholar

Charles W. Calomiris
Arthur F. Burns Scholar in
 Economics

Liz Cheney
Visiting Fellow

Veronique de Rugy
Research Fellow

Thomas Donnelly
Resident Fellow

Nicholas Eberstadt
Henry Wendt Scholar in Political
 Economy

Eric M. Engen
Resident Scholar

Mark Falcoff
Resident Scholar Emeritus

J. Michael Finger
Resident Scholar

Gerald R. Ford
Distinguished Fellow

John C. Fortier
Research Fellow

David Frum
Resident Fellow

Ted Gayer
Visiting Scholar

Reuel Marc Gerecht
Resident Fellow

Newt Gingrich
Senior Fellow

Jack Goldsmith
Visiting Scholar

Robert A. Goldwin
Resident Scholar

Scott Gottlieb
Resident Fellow

Michael S. Greve
John G. Searle Scholar

Robert W. Hahn
Resident Scholar; Director,
 AEI-Brookings Joint Center
 for Regulatory Studies

Kevin A. Hassett
Resident Scholar; Director,
 Economic Policy Studies

Steven F. Hayward
F. K. Weyerhaeuser Fellow

Robert B. Helms
Resident Scholar; Director,
 Health Policy Studies

Frederick M. Hess
Resident Scholar; Director,
 Education Policy Studies

R. Glenn Hubbard
Visiting Scholar

Leon R. Kass
Hertog Fellow

Herbert G. Klein
National Fellow

Jeane J. Kirkpatrick
Senior Fellow

Marvin H. Kosters
Resident Scholar

Irving Kristol
Senior Fellow

Randall S. Kroszner
Visiting Scholar

Desmond Lachman
Resident Fellow

Michael A. Ledeen
Freedom Scholar

James R. Lilley
Senior Fellow

Lawrence B. Lindsey
Visiting Scholar

John R. Lott Jr.
Resident Scholar

John H. Makin
Resident Scholar; Director,
 Fiscal Policy Studies

Allan H. Meltzer
Visiting Scholar

Joshua Muravchik
Resident Scholar

Charles Murray
W. H. Brady Scholar

Michael Novak
George Frederick Jewett Scholar
 in Religion, Philosophy, and Public
 Policy; Director, Social and Political
 Studies

Norman J. Ornstein
Resident Scholar

Richard Perle
Resident Fellow

Alex J. Pollock
Resident Fellow

Sarath Rajapatirana
Visiting Scholar

Michael Rubin
Resident Scholar

Sally Satel
Resident Scholar

William Schneider
Resident Fellow

Daniel Shaviro
Visiting Scholar

Joel Schwartz
Visiting Scholar

J. Gregory Sidak
Resident Scholar

Radek Sikorski
Resident Fellow; Executive
 Director, New Atlantic Initiative

Christina Hoff Sommers
Resident Scholar

Fred Thompson
Visiting Fellow

Peter J. Wallison
Resident Fellow

Scott Wallsten
Resident Scholar

Ben J. Wattenberg
Senior Fellow

John Yoo
Visiting Fellow

Karl Zinsmeister
J. B. Fuqua Fellow; Editor,
 The American Enterprise